Wartime
SCRAPBOOK

Wartime
SCRAPBOOK

Compiled and edited by
Barbara Dixon

COLLINS & BROWN

First published in Great Britain in 2005 by
Collins & Brown
The Chrysalis Building
Bramley Road
London
W10 6SP

An imprint of **Chrysalis** Books Group plc

Published in association with
The National Magazine Company Limited.
Good Housekeeping is a registered trademark of The National
Magazine Company Limited.

ISBN: 1 84340 262 9

1 2 3 4 5 6 7 8 9

Designed by Simon Daley
Text and material compiled by Barbara Dixon
from *Good Housekeeping* archives 1939–47.

Reproduction by Anorax Imaging Ltd, England
Printed and bound by G.Canale & C spa, Italy

Contents

When home lights gleam again!

Speed the day when peace returns and "SKY-LINE" Kitchen Tools, with their familiar bright green ivory – banded handles, pre-war sparkle and gleaming plate, are again in ample supply to brighten British homes and lighten labour everywhere.

Issued by Platers & Stampers Limited.

On the
HOME FRONT

By the middle of 1940 over 20 per cent of the male population of the British Isles were in the services, and it fell to women to take on the role of head of the household. They had to deal with rationing, making do and mending, saving and budgeting, and putting a brave face on things for the family. They were urged by the government to keep cheerful, have courage and cope with the difficulties of day-to-day living by keeping the home fires burning – but not literally, coal was in short supply and ingenuity was called for to provide heat and fuel in the house.

Ration books and coupons became the subject of magazine articles, with advice on getting the most out of what they would buy, while shortages of many familiar items brought suggestions for inventive substitutes. As the war progressed, families were separated and queuing became a part of life, but the fighting spirit prevailed as much at home as it did on the battlefields.

Running a HOME—

By Phyllis L. Garbutt, A.R.I.C.

TAXES

CLOTHIN

SAVING

HOLIDAYS

A QUESTION that is puzzling many a bride or bride-to-be these days. The answer depends on four things: your standard of living, the district in which you live or propose to live, your husband's employment and the extent of your entertaining. All these and other considerations must be borne in mind when planning a workable budget. Neglect of this preparatory arithmetic has shipwrecked many a home, so, if you would be wise, think out your finances now.

First—organise the pounds.
Next—plan the shillings.
Lastly—look after the pence.

Organising the Pounds

Even if you do not know your future income exactly, you probably know enough to be able to get to work. Underestimate rather than over-estimate; if you hope for an income of £600, plan for £500. It is always easier to expand a budget than contract it.

First work out your *net* income: that is the sum you will have left after income tax is deducted. Pay-as-you-earn income tax has made this job easier for nearly everybody; but if your fiancé is a professional man, or working on his own account, you will find the following figures (based on the present rate of income tax) helpful.

Income tax due from a married man (no children, no dependent relatives, no life insurance) earning £500 a year.

Earned income . . .		£500
Allowances :		
$\frac{1}{10}$ earned income . .	£50	
Personal allowance .	80	
Add for wife . .	60	
	—	
		190
Taxable income . . .		310
On which tax is paid on £165 at		
6s. 6d.		53 12 6
£145 at		
10s.		72 10 0
		£126 2 6

leaving a net income of £373 17s. 6d.

Put your net income down on paper, and then begin to think about percentages. What *proportion* should you spend on rent—or, if you are going to be lucky enough to own your own house or wise enough to buy it on some spread-over payment system—on rates and Schedule A? What *proportion* should go to the running expenses of the house —food, wages for domestic help, lighting, heating,

28

laundry and so on? What *proportion* to clothin and personal expenses? And how can you provi for those "unexpected" expenses which w always turn up whether expected or not—illnes house repairs and so on?

The following are what are called recommende percentage figures. These can only serve as general guide, remember: you may find you hav to deviate from them quite appreciably when comes to working out your own scheme. T "savings" figure will probably include some li insurance, one of the best of all forms of saving for newly-married couple; or, if and when Soci Security comes, it must include the sum (in the ca of a two-person family with only one wage-earne just under £10 a year) which will have to be pa in contribution to the scheme.

25% for rent, mortgage or maintenance of propert rates and taxes.

40% for all household expenses, food, wages, ligh ing, cooking, laundry, cleaning materials, newals, heating, telephone.

15% for clothing and personal expenses generall

Watching the Pennie

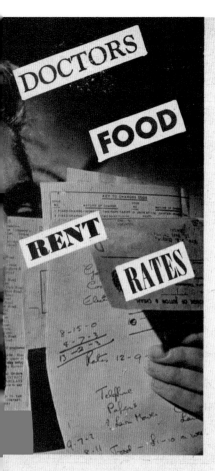

What does it COST?

you need; rates should be ascertained if they will figure in your budget. Armed with this, and as much other information as possible, you can get to work on your outline.

When the time comes to put your scheme into operation, you are bound to find some modifications are necessary. Putting any plan into practice is harder than any amount of theorising. But don't worry—revise your scheme, and for any additional expense on one item, make a corresponding cut somewhere else. The only thing that should not be cut, unless it is humanly impossible to do otherwise, is the margin for the "unexpected."

Planning the Shillings

What should be allowed for housekeeping? It is here that the shillings are mainly spent. First it must be clearly decided what items housekeeping should cover. It will, of course, include the cost of food and cleaning materials, probably wages of any domestic help, and laundry. Lighting, heating and telephone may also be included: these items will alter your allocation considerably, but in any case the point should be clearly decided beforehand. During the war, and probably for some time to come, Government subsidies and controls for many essential foods, together with the limited supply of luxuries, make it possible to cater for much the same total amount as in pre-war days. Less is of necessity spent at the butcher's and at the dairy; more in most cases at the grocer's. The shortage of fruit, too, means that many households spend far less now than they used to on green-groceries, particularly if they grow most of their own vegetables.

For a typical middle-class household a sum of about 15s. per head weekly for food is still an adequate allowance, and it is possible to manage reasonably well on less. More, of course, will be spent if luxury foods are included, or if the housewife is not a careful caterer. It is sound housekeeping to purchase as much dairy produce as rations allow, to provide plenty of vegetables and to offer fruit, too, when it is available.

When housekeeping expenses are too high, don't cut those items, but look rather to the grocer's account, where extravagance, as a rule, first shows itself. Even to-day it is still possible to over-spend on canned and prepared foods, biscuits, etc.

Look after the Pence

This is not always easy, for they slip away so readily on trifles. Try keeping a record of expenditure—every single item—for a week. Unless you are very exceptional and exercise great self-control, you will probably be painfully surprised at the result. Often the purchases involved are small; but their cost mounts alarmingly, and if you multiply that cost by fifty-two, for the fifty-two weeks of the year, you may find that the pence are running away with the shillings and even the tens of pounds.

5% for recreation, holidays, charity, etc.
10% for saving.
5% as margin for unexpected expenses.

If your net income is as high as £500 a year, the figures, worked out in these proportions, would therefore be :
£125 for rent, etc.
£200 for all household expenses.
£75 for clothing and personal expenses.
£25 for recreation, holidays, charity, etc.
£50 for saving.
£25 for unexpected expenses.
If your net income is under £500 you may find difficulty in keeping close to this apportionment. Your rent (or property expenses) must be carefully considered, your domestic help cut to a minimum, your "personal expenses" worked out to cover the cost of your husband's travelling to and from his work, if that is necessary, and of his meals taken away from home. You will need, before you begin serious budgeting, an idea of the rents or prices prevailing in the district for the kind of house or flat

△ As 1944 came to a close with no sign of an end to the war, *Good Housekeeping* offered advice to housewives on how to simplify and organize their finances and begin serious budgeting.

IS HE THE BEE IN YOUR BONNET?

DID YOU HEAR THE SHOPKEEPER SAY 'NO MORE WHEN THIS STOCK'S GONE?'

GIFTS FOR HITLER, Mrs. T?..

We know that you're out for victory, Mrs. T.

There's not a more patriotic woman in the place—not one who's pulling her weight better on committees and in working parties.

But there's one other matter, Mrs. T.—*what is your money doing behind your back?*

Some of it goes on things you could do without, Mrs. T. Harmless little extras, you say? Oh, no—*not* harmless. Every pound you needlessly spend might just as well be labelled "A present to Hitler from Mrs. T. to make the war longer." That's the plain truth, Mrs. T.

Go on with your good work for the country, but make your money do a real job too. Help to win the war quickly by never buying anything unless it's really necessary.

Invest in Defence Bonds steadily up to the £1,000 limit. You'll be helping to make a new world all the sooner—and you'll have a bigger stake in it.

3% DEFENCE BONDS

"LET'S BE THE WISE ONES, DOROTHY!

I know there's loads of things we want. But, darling, don't let's spend our savings before it's worth it. This war's got to be won first and then it's going to take a bit of clearing up—I mean materials will be short, lots of priority needs will have to come first. What'll happen if there is a scramble to spend? We won't get what we want, and we'll probably have to pay high prices. So what I say is—let's save and wait!"

YOU'LL BE GLAD YOU KEPT ON SAVING

△ To meet the costs of the war a National Savings Campaign began in November 1939, and people were encouraged to save, save, save. However, the swastika-decorated Squander Bug encouraged them to spend, spend, spend.

▷ Cutting down on household expenditure ensured there was money available to save – this article from January 1942 offers helpful advice.

Save, Don't Squander

Budgeting for Victory

ʜNERAL MAID

ʜt year's average
ʜekly wages £1 10s. 0d.

This may not sound very heavy, but with the children now all of school age, it might be practicable to manage either with part-time daily maid or occasional charwoman. Latter plan resolved on.

ʜolved for this year 15s. 0d.

ʜNDRYWORK

ʜt year's average
ʜekly cost 10s. 0d.

Laundry charges have risen, but if " smalls " are washed at home, it should only be necessary to allow for sheets, table-cloths, large bath towels and possibly men's shirts. Resolved to cut expenditure on laundrywork.

ʜolved for this year 7s. 0d.

ʜANING MATERIALS

ʜt year's average
ʜekly expenditure 3s. 6d.

This figure indicates rather extravagant use of cleaning materials. Resolved, therefore, to cut expenditure.

ʜolved for this year 2s. 6d.

ʜL—COAL, GAS, ELECTRICITY

ʜt year's average
ʜekly cost 15s. 0d.

Strict fuel economy is demanded by the Government, and still smaller consumption must be aimed at by every household. Cut of at least 2s. 6d. decided.

ʜolved for this year 12s. 6d.

ʜLIDAYS AND AMUSEMENTS

ʜt year's average
ʜekly expenditure 15s. 0d.

These expenses must be still further cut. Suggest a reduction of at least 5s. per week.

ʜolved for this year 10s. 0d.

ʜNEWALS

ʜt year's average
ʜekly cost 5s. 0d.

This amount will probably be automatically cut in most households on account of the increasing shortage of supplies.

ʜolved for this year 2s. 6d.

CHEMIST'S BILL

Last year's weekly
average 6s. 0d.

It is surprising how much we spend quite unthinkingly at the chemist's, but this also will probably be automatically reduced by the shortage of toilet requisites and other non-essential supplies.

Resolved for this year 4s. 0d.

CAR, CLEANING, GARAGE, TAX, etc.

Last year's average
weekly expenditure 17s. 6d.

Petrol-rationing means that a car can be little used, and thus running costs are automatically reduced. On the other hand, taxation and insurance are heavy. It is impossible to estimate running costs and repairs accurately, but it was resolved to decrease costs by laying up car for first three months of the year.

Resolved for this year 15s. 0d.

LOCAL BUS FARES, etc.

Last year's average
weekly allowance 5s. 0d.

This only allows of occasional bus fares, but it might be possible with care to cut them a little.

Resolved for this year 4s. 6d.

TELEPHONE

Last year's average
weekly expenditure 5s. 0d.

It is not always possible to cut this expense, but there are people who still make very careless use of the telephone. Take the hint!

Resolved for this year 4s. 0d.

CLOTHES AND SMALL PERSONAL EXPENSES

Last year's average
weekly allowance £2 0s. 0d.

Clothes rationing effectively reduced expenditure on this item after May last. It should be possible to plan an effective cut here this year.

Resolved for this year, £1 10s. 0d.

IN many households it will, of course, be necessary to make separate provision for husband's, or, in these days, possibly for one's own business expenses, such as season ticket, lunches, etc.

BY pruning expenditure in this way our imaginary family planned to save something like £3 per week. You may not be able to increase your savings quite so spectacularly, perhaps because you have already made very heavy cuts or because your income is very much less. Whatever your individual circumstances, though, do remember it is the small cuts here and there that add up and make something worthwhile, although even with the best will in the world, of course, one must be prepared for the fact that some unexpected contingency may lead to unexpected expenses.

HAVING decided to save to the utmost, you must next consider the most practical way of keeping to your resolution, and also decide what you are going to do with your savings. Many ingenious ways of saving have been thought out and publicised, and we must all adopt the most appropriate or attractive method. Many people find one of the group schemes a great boon, for combined effort is always an advantage, and the very fact that one's friends, neighbours and fellow-workers are all taking part in this great savings drive is a real incentive. There is the National Savings Certificate Cycle Scheme. This is very popular with the small investor, who subscribes a certain sum per week towards the purchase of Saving Certificates. Other schemes for the purchase of Defence Bonds by instalments are also in operation, and full details can be obtained from the National Savings Movement. There is, however, no doubt that a firm resolution on the part of everyone in the family, including children, to save some definite sum every week or month, is much more satisfactory for most people than casual saving, which is very apt to become less and less as time goes on.

* Before you travel, ask, " Is it necessary ? "

How is the POINTS Scheme Working?

GOOD HOUSEKEEPING reviews this great Rationing Experiment

◁ With food imports severely curtailed, rationing started in January 1940. In addition to their weekly ration, everyone received 16 points a month to spend on a selected range of foods as they wished.

▷ In June 1941 clothing was rationed and an annual allowance of 66 coupons was issued to every man, woman and child.

Points Means Coupons

CAREFUL LAUNDERING

Legitimate wear and tear make a bad enough hole in your clothes coupons, so don't let careless laundering do more. During washing a lot of damage can be done of which you may be quite blissfully ignorant, but which will just as surely weaken clothes as shrinkage or other obvious wear. Indeed, it has been proved that with care the average life of fabrics can be increased by as much as 25 per cent.

DON'T

—*let things get so dirty before washing* that drastic methods are needed to cleanse them.

—*be unnecessarily rough with clothes.* Cleanse as far as possible by gentle squeezing. If you must rub, rub the affected parts lightly. Be particularly careful with woollies and artificial silks, for the former can soon be badly "felted" and the latter injured by careless handling.

—*stretch and pull artificial silk* when wet, for the fibres are weaker then.

—*use too much hot water for coloured articles*—luke-warm is best.

—*use too much soap or soda.* Too much of either actually hinders rather than helps cleansing, so avoid regular use of powders containing an excess of alkali or bleaching agent. Pure laundry soap or soap flakes are a good choice.

—*leave articles too long in your washing machine*, if you possess one. To avoid this necessity, sort the clothes carefully, and wash the cleanest together, allowing the minimum time for cleansing. If lightly soiled and more heavily soiled articles are washed together, the tendency, of course, is to keep them in the water too long.

—*use bleaching agents unnecessarily.* The best and most harmless way is to bleach things out-of-doors in sunshine and fresh air. Spread out on the lawn and sprinkle now and again with a watering-can, as moisture is an essential condition to quick bleaching. A powder with bleaching properties can be used occasionally for white cotton and linen articles. Bleaches other than hydrogen peroxide should not be used for silks and woollens, although a faintly blue final rinse often helps if they have developed a yellowish tinge.

—*iron clothes when they are too damp,* for in this way you will waste electricity or gas. Dry them to the correct degree of dampness and then roll up for an hour or so, to spread the moisture evenly. Place articles carefully on the ironing-board and iron the way of the selvedge.

—*iron in creases of table linen*, etc., or if you do, vary the folding, so as to prolong their life.

—*put starched things away for any length of time.* If you do, you are likely to cause serious rotting and deterioration.

—*damp down rayons and don't use too hot an iron*, as this may melt some of the surface fibres and do irreparable damage.

Save Those Coupons

SAVES COUPONS

By Phyllis L. Garbutt, A.I.C.

DON'T

—use a hot iron for woollens. They should be pressed rather than ironed, that is to say, the iron should be lifted up and put down, rather than glided along the material.

DO

—remember to wash stockings every day if possible.

—look out for small tears and mend them immediately.

—remove stains immediately. The longer they are left the more firmly set they become.

—adopt the simplest methods of treatment possible.

—keep woollies under water as far as possible while washing. Lifting them in and out of the water while washing causes unnecessary strain.

—use soft water where possible. Rain-water is, of course, ideal. Otherwise use water run through a chemical plant or carefully soften it with soda, as directed last month.

—remember skirts, frocks and unlined coats can be washed successfully at home.

—use your wringer carefully. More damage is caused by careless wringing than by any other single factor. Fold the clothes roughly lengthwise before passing through the rollers; and to avoid breaking buttons and possibly cutting the material, see that there are several thicknesses of the material adjoining the buttons, to protect them as they pass through.

—take care when pegging articles out to dry. Hang garments from the shoulders or place on a coat hanger. Hang stockings from the toes. Remember to stretch woollens when wet to their original shape, and to dry jumpers and cardigans on a flat surface.

—remember to air things thoroughly. But on no account leave them indefinitely in an airing cupboard, for this can often rot the fabrics. After airing they should be kept in a cool, dry cupboard.

—place freshly laundered linen at the bottom of the pile, so that articles are used as far as possible in rotation.

—remember, when mending, not to darn too tightly and so cause unnecessary strain and pull.

△ With new clothes rationed, learning to care for what you had became paramount and many helpful articles appeared with sage advice, such as this one from September 1943.

I'M STILL GOING STRONG I'M JURY HOLLOW-WARE

Like most good things I'm in short supply at the moment, but as soon as the happy days of peace return I shall be freely available and you will find me everywhere.

A Hint

To preserve your JURY Hollow-ware don't scrape, but soak.

JURY HOLLOWARE (STEVENS) LTD.
BRIERLEY HILL . . . . . STAFFS.

Sorry— but there are not enough of these *Anglepoise* lamps to go round now

One of the pleasures of the happier days ahead

WE apologise for the shortage of Anglepoise Lamps—the marvellous 1,001-angle lamps which made life so easy in pre-war days. We dislike having to disappoint our many friends, but war's stern necessity compels us to do so.

But the Anglepoise—that marvellous 1,001-angle lamp—is well worth waiting for and that happy day will come (sooner than many realise) when supplies will be ample and the Anglepoise will be easing the eyes and adding to the amenities of a peaceful England. Till then . . .

Pat. all countries

SOME OF THE 1001 ANGLES TAKEN BY THIS WONDERFUL LAMP

Sole Makers :
HERBERT TERRY & SONS, Ltd., Redditch
London · Manchester · Birmingham

The TERRY *Anglepoise* LAMP
Scarce now—but well worth waiting for

Tanks can't run on toasters

—So G.E.C. Toasters are temporarily unobtainable, the same as most other of the Company's Household Electric Appliances, to reappear after the war in new and better designs, to give you a fresh appreciation of how much electricity can do in the home; but until then metal and labour must be diverted to priority requirements.

G.E.C.
HOUSEHOLD ELECTRIC APPLIANCES

△ Although many familiar items were in short supply, manufacturers continued advertising throughout the war to remind readers that they would be back once peacetime came.
▷ In February 1942 soap was rationed to 3oz a month and the Good Housekeeping Institute tackled queries from readers on coping with the shortages.

Making Do

Now *that* Soap *is* Rationed

By
P. L. GARBUTT
Director of Good
Housekeeping Institute

This is the soap allowance for a family of four, apportioned equally between soap flakes, laundry soap, No. 1 soap powder, and toilet soap

Small wonder that there are always laundry problems in the Institute mail, now that soap is rationed and laundries often will not accept new customers. It is not easy to make the soap last out, especially where there are children, but you can help yourself quite a lot by taking a little trouble.

Here are some of the questions we have been asked recently, and among them may be your problem, too. If not, write and let us know your difficulty.

Query I : Soap Rationing

The first question comes from the mother of a family who is anxious to know how she can best soften water and so save her soap ration. This question is published because it is a difficulty shared to some extent by all readers just now.

Our Advice

(1) Install a mains softener if, like our questioner, you live in a hard-water district, are able to secure a model, and can meet the cost. (We ascertained, by the way, that models were available at the time of writing.)

(2) Alternatively, collect and use rain-water for washing and household cleaning purposes, if possible.

(3) If, for one reason or another, the above suggestions are impracticable, use soda to soften the water, but be *very* careful not to use too much, especially when washing delicate articles. Actually, *very little* indeed is required, far less than most people imagine.

The simplest and safest way of using washing soda is to dissolve 1 oz. in a pint of water and bottle this solution, adding about 1 tablespoonful to every gallon of hot water for every 5 degrees of hardness, i.e., for water of 20 degrees of hardness, add 4 tablespoonfuls per gallon. (Your water company will tell

you the degree of hardness of your water supply.) Place requisite quantity of soda solution in a bowl before running in the hot water, and leave for a moment or two, if possible, so that it has a chance of reacting with the hardness before you add the soap. This may sound a little complicated, but is actually very simple once you have ascertained the hardness of your water and measured up the bowl or bath you generally use. Adding the required amount of soda *before* the soap will, indeed, soon become a habit, and a very worthwhile one, which may save you a really big proportion of your soap ration, possibly as much as a quarter.

Query II : Washing Woollens

"After using lukewarm water for years, I have been told that woollens can be washed successfully with boiling water. I should like to have your opinion."

Our Advice

We explained to our reader that there are several satisfactory ways of washing woollens, and that one involves the use of practically boiling water. This method gives very good results, provided care is taken not to immerse the wool in cold water immediately after the hot. If, however,

articles are left in the washing water until cool enough to handle, and rinsing water of about the same temperature is used, no harm will result. Many people prefer to wash woollens in this way rather than in the more usually accepted one, involving the use of water at about blood heat.

Things to avoid when washing woollens are : (1) rubbing, which very soon causes felting and shrinkage; (2) extremes of temperature; (3) the use of strong alkalies, such as soda, all of which are injurious.

Query III : Substitutes for Laundry Starch

"Can you tell me of any satisfactory substitute for laundry starch, which is now unprocurable in my district?"

Our Advice

We explained that satisfactory substitutes for laundry starch are farinaceous substances, such as flour, rice-water, etc., all of which are valuable foodstuffs and should, therefore, not be used for other than feeding purposes in war-time. For thin muslin articles gum arabic is sometimes used, but this only gives very slight stiffening, and may not be easy to obtain at the present time. In any case, it is unsuitable for heavy articles.

* Keep a daily check on your dustbin.

Colour isn't rationed

Little Christmas trees may be more possible, in your district, than one big one

Garland your mirrors with greenstuff, make them gay with queer animals. The children will enjoy cutting newspaper giraffes and brown-paper bunnies

A Cold Christmas

Scraps of bright paper can be saved for star-shaped place-mats. Add a centrepiece of holly and fir-cones, candle-lit

By Christine Palmer

paper on sale; pick it up when you can, but keep the tinsel in a dark place to save its brightest glitter till the last.

Make a centrepiece for your table of evergreens and berries. The children can begin to search now for ivy and fir-cones and the bright uneatable berries. Winter greenstuff will last a long time if kept in water. The children can begin cutting out paper animals, too; but you'll add to the excitement if you don't tell them what the animals are for. Then on Christmas Eve, when the last stocking has been filled to overflowing with your ingenuity and thought, you can transform the living-room into a crazy, colourful, lovely background for fun.

THIS year you won't be able to make cakes and Christmas puddings and mincemeat weeks in advance. This year you may not be having a big family gathering at all. But colour and fun and goodwill aren't rationed, and there is no need to be lonely if you have a roof over your head. Could you join forces with another family, share your food, fuel and cheerfulness? Could you open your front door to some exiled strangers, and show them that the traditional English Christmas doesn't depend entirely on a groaning board, but has some deeper warmth as well?

If you can, write to the Chaplain or Welfare Officer of any troops stationed near you. Tell him clearly of the hospitality you can offer. Then set to work to make your home as attractive and un-everyday as possible.

Bring out brightly coloured pieces of china, fabric, paper and ribbon and see what you can evolve from them. Use colour boldly and gaily. Tree-branches can be made dramatic and beautiful with splashes of shoe-white: odd pieces of "Cellophane," scraps of velvet, and shaggy flowers made from loops of coloured string can all be used for decoration. There will be some tinsel ribbon and some coloured

No tree at all? Then get a branch of plum or cherry, paint it with the stuff you use for white shoes, and decorate it with anything bright you can find

△ Since many families would be separated and food would be in short supply, a little imagination was called for to make the home festive for Christmas, as supplied in this article from December 1943.

Crochet, insertion or ricrac braid joining four unused table-napkins to make a tea-cloth.

Cushion-covers—patchwork, plain material with a strip of vivi... embroidery, or what-have-you...

For the goer-up-to-town, a holdall made from hessian. Detailed instructions on page 100.

Set of store jars—any screw-top jars you can collect, their lids enamelled in any colour.

Shopping bag which folds up to a neat pochette. Detailed instructions and diagram are on page 100.

Aprons, always welcomed if they are dainty enough. Two or more materials add to the gaiety.

Make your Gifts

Thrifty Advice

For travelling book-
worms—a cover made
from scraps of leather,
Lancaster cloth or cretonne.

Boon to the
housewife—a peg
bag mounted on a coat-
hanger, to slip along the line.

Boxes and tins,
always useful to
everybody, covered with wallpaper,
furnishing fabric or enamel.

Tea-cosy for a
household present.
Make it of patchwork, and
large enough for the family pot.

foot-muff for your mother or
unt. Best parts of an old blanket
rug for decoration and padding.

Coal-mit made from black velvet,
or polishing mit made from any
bits of firm material, well padded.

△ Christmas 1943: making your own and recycling just
about anything were popular ways of producing presents
when money and luxuries were in short supply.

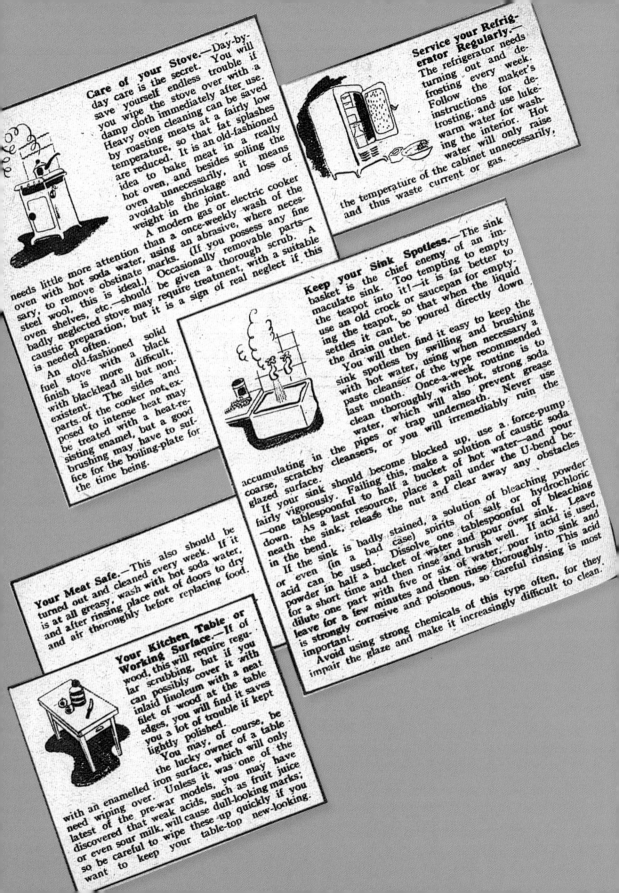

Care of your Stove.

Day-by-day care is the secret. You will save yourself endless trouble if you wipe the stove over with a damp cloth immediately after use. Heavy oven cleaning can be saved by roasting meats at a fairly low temperature, so that fat splashes are reduced. It is an old-fashioned idea to bake meat in a really hot oven, and besides soiling the oven unnecessarily, it means avoidable shrinkage and loss of weight in the joint.

A modern gas or electric cooker needs little more attention than a once-weekly wash of the oven with hot soda water. To remove obstinate marks, using an abrasive, where necessary, to remove obstinate marks, using an abrasive, where necessary, steel wool, this is ideal.) (If you possess any fine oven shelves, etc.—should be given a thorough scrub. A badly neglected stove may require treatment, with a suitable caustic preparation, but it is a sign of real neglect if this is needed often.

An old-fashioned solid fuel stove with a black finish is more difficult, with blacklead all but non-existent. The sides and parts of the cooker not exposed to intense heat may be treated with a heat-resisting enamel, but a good brushing may have to suffice for the boiling-plate for the time being.

Service your Refrigerator Regularly.

The refrigerator needs turning out and defrosting every week. Follow the maker's instructions for defrosting, and use lukewarm water for washing the interior. Hot water will only raise the temperature of the cabinet unnecessarily, and thus waste current or gas.

Keep your Sink Spotless.

The sink basket is the chief enemy of an immaculate sink. Too tempting to empty the teapot into it!—it is far better to use an old crock or saucepan for emptying the teapot, so that when the liquid settles it can be poured directly down the drain outlet.

You will then find it easy to keep the sink spotless by swilling and brushing with hot water, using when necessary a paste cleanser of the type recommended last month. Once-a-week routine is to clean thoroughly with hot, strong soda water, which will also prevent grease accumulating in the pipes, or trap underneath. Never use coarse, scratchy cleansers, or you will irremediably ruin the glazed surface.

If your sink should become blocked up, use a force-pump fairly vigorously. Failing this, make a solution of caustic soda—one tablespoonful to half a bucket of hot water—and pour down. As a last resource, place a pail under the U-bend beneath the sink, release the nut and clear away any obstacles in the bend.

If the sink is badly stained, a solution of bleaching powder or even (in a bad case) spirits of salt or hydrochloric acid can be used. Dissolve one tablespoonful of bleaching powder in half a bucket of water and pour over sink. If acid is used, dilute one part with five or six of water, pour into sink and leave for a few minutes and then rinse thoroughly. This acid is strongly corrosive and poisonous, so careful rinsing is most important.

Avoid using strong chemicals of this type often, for they impair the glaze and make it increasingly difficult to clean.

Your Meat Safe.

This also should be turned out and cleaned every week. If it is at all greasy, wash with hot soda water, and after rinsing place out of doors to dry and air thoroughly before replacing food.

Your Kitchen Table or Working Surface.

If of wood, this will require regular scrubbing, but if you can possibly cover it with a neat inlaid linoleum with a neat filet of wood at the table edges, you will find it saves you a lot of trouble if kept lightly polished.

You may, of course, be the lucky owner of a table with an enamelled iron surface, which will only need wiping over. Unless it was one of the latest of the pre-war models, you may have discovered that weak acids, such as fruit juice or even sour milk, will cause dull-looking marks; so be careful to wipe these up quickly if you want to keep your table-top new-looking.

By 1943 more than 100,000 women worked in some capacity in the railway industry, but for all working women housework still had to be tackled

◁▷ The nation might have been at war, but cleanliness was next to godliness and appearances had to be kept up.

Keeping Up Appearances

Looking to the Future

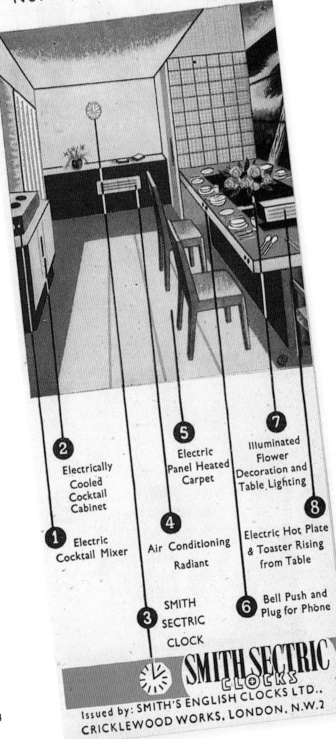

THE ALL ELECTRIC HOME OF THE FUTURE

No. 2 THE DINING ROOM

2 Electrically Cooled Cocktail Cabinet

1 Electric Cocktail Mixer

5 Electric Panel Heated Carpet

4 Air Conditioning Radiant

3 SMITH SECTRIC CLOCK

7 Illuminated Flower Decoration and Table Lighting

8 Electric Hot Plate & Toaster Rising from Table

6 Bell Push and Plug for Phone

SMITH SECTRIC CLOCKS

Issued by: SMITH'S ENGLISH CLOCKS LTD., CRICKLEWOOD WORKS, LONDON, N.W.2

◁▷ In 1945, as the war drew to a close, and with it the prospect of a return to normality, people began to look to the future. The all-electric dining room (left) was a very advanced ideal, while *Good Housekeeping*'s new-look kitchen (right) was practical and efficient.

TO-MORROW'S KITCHEN ?

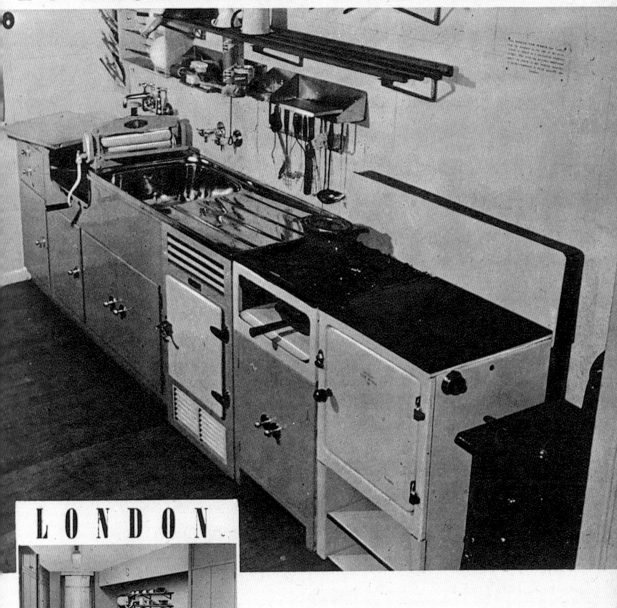

LONDON

All the main working units are placed in one line, with a roomy clothes-drying cabinet on the right

HERE and on the following two pages are illustrated some new kitchens. Not only in London, but all over the country, keen brains are working to make "the workshop of the home" a lighter, brighter and more efficient place. Look carefully at these pictures, compare them with your own post-war plans and aims. For such kitchens are no longer in the luxury class ; after the war they can be installed, whole or in part, in your own existing home. Standardisation—pre-fabrication—these twin terms of to-day may well transform your home to-morrow.

PARENTING
& Health

Once their husbands had gone off to war, and faced with the unwelcome challenge of suddenly becoming a single-parent family, many mothers turned to *Good Housekeeping* for advice on aspects of childcare and health. Its pages carried bulletins from the Ministries of Food and Health, reminding readers of the welfare schemes and immunisation available, while the resident Children's Doctor offered advice on readers' problems.

At home, one of the consequences of war was an increase in pre- and extra-marital sex, venereal disease and illegitimacy and in 1942 the Ministry of Health pulled no punches in launching their 'awareness of VD' campaign. With some children born illegitimately and given up for adoption, others orphaned, and others still neglected, the NSPCC and Dr Barnardo's were organisations vital to the care of such children and the magazine carried appeals and articles about their plight.

Good Housekeeping

Christmas Number

6

Specially written story by Eleanor Farjeon

F. H. GRISEWOOD : WALTER KARIG : MARJORIE HESSELL TILTMAN

CHRISTMAS CATERING BY THE INSTITUTE

Brighter Breakfasts

THE mornings are brighter . . . Why not brighter breakfasts, too? Ringing the changes is not at all difficult, especially with our old friends carrots and potatoes to help. And we can well do with more of these foods, now that the rations in fat and sugar are back to where they were before their winter increase.

Simple — but different. *Potato Floddies* are quick to prepare and are especially appetising if cooked in the fat left over from bacon. Grate raw potatoes into a basin. Mix in enough flour to make a thick batter, season to taste, drop spoonfuls of the mixture into a pan of hot fat. Fry on both sides. *Another novelty* is slices of cooked carrot fried with bacon. Their cheery colour reminds you of "bacon and tomatoes," but their flavour is new and delicious. *What about a cereal?* Stale bread, cut in cubes and baked, makes a crunchy, nourishing breakfast cereal. Use the heat left in the oven when you finish the main cooking.

To the mother of a baby. Your baby's growth may be stunted and his vitality impoverished if you don't see he gets his proper vitamins. The Government provides blackcurrant juice for all babies up to two years of age, and cod-liver oil for all children up to six — holders of the green ration book. Blackcurrant juice is as rich in Vitamin C as orange juice is; and cod-liver oil — because of its Vitamins A and D — is of vital importance to growing babies. So if you are not yet taking advantage of the Government's schemes *please go now,* or write, to your Local Food Office and they will tell you how to get your baby's ration of vitamins.

Please carry your shopping home. The Government are asking your tradesmen to pool their deliveries. This is to save petrol, tyres, wear and tear of vehicles, and, above all, manpower. So your butcher, grocer and fishmonger may arrange to divide your district, each taking one section and delivering other tradesmen's goods with his own. Even at this, and with the best will in the world, there may be only one or two deliveries a week, and these may not be on the days you prefer. Housekeeping will be so much simpler, therefore, if you carry your shopping home, *and you will be taking still another pull on the life-line to victory.*

LET'S TALK ABOUT PROTECTIVE

FOOD

There are certain foods which have a wonderful power to keep you in health. They are what Dieticians call "protective" foods, and among the most valuable of these are wheatmeal bread, green vegetables, carrots, potatoes. The important thing is to have a good helping — or better still, two good helpings — of some or other of these foods every day. Carrots have an unusual claim on your attention, at this time of year especially, because as well as protecting you against colds and infection, they help you to see in the dark.

QUESTIONS YOU ASK

My skin is not as good as it used to be; I think it's lack of fruit.

It's the Vitamin C in the fruit that is so good for your skin — and for your health. But you get exactly the same vitamin in vegetables. Remember, however, that you must have *extra* vegetable to make up for the missing fruit. Everyone needs at least 1,000 units of Vitamin C every day. Here is a brief list to guide you:

		Vitamin C Units
Spinach	4 ozs. cooked =	700
Broccoli	" " =	600
Turnip Tops	" " =	480
Cabbage	" " =	300
Swedes	" " =	260
Potatoes	" " =	240
Watercress	½ oz. raw =	150
Spinach	" " =	150
Cabbage	" " =	100
Parsley	" " =	70

Note how much richer in Vitamin C are raw vegetables.

Then there are carrots. Although not a good source of Vitamin C, carrots provide other elements which clear the skin and improve its texture. A good plan therefore — and a plan for everyone who values health — is to have a raw vegetable salad (based on shredded cabbage heart or other green stuff, watercress and grated carrot); or cooked carrots; or an extra helping of green vegetables *as well as* your usual vegetables, every day.

We do miss breakfast marmalade.

We are posting you a recipe for Orange-peel Marmalade. But have you tried rhubarb jam? It has a refreshing tart-sweet flavour — that little appetising "kick" you like at breakfast.

Can you give me a new soup recipe?

Here's a delicious one: *Golden Barley Soup.* Grate or mince 2 lbs. of carrots, put with 1 small teacupful of barley into 1 quart of water and simmer for 2½ hours. Roll a piece of margarine the size of a walnut in 1 tablespoonful of flour and stir it into the soup. Cook fast for 8 minutes, season with pepper and salt. Serves 4 or 5

Just why is national wheatmeal bread good for you?

Mainly because it is a protective food, as well as being very nourishing. It gives you a supply of the B Vitamins — those that keep the nerves and digestive system in good order. Did you know you could also get national wheatmeal flour? It makes the most delicious buns, scones and cakes.

Now, Listen Carefully...

Let's talk about _your_ child's FOOD

We women at the Ministry of Food who assist Lord Woolton in answering your letters, share his deep interest in helping you to feed your children properly in war-time. Our hearts are in it : many of us have children of our own and, like yourselves, we are practical housewives. We know how worrying it is when you can't buy foods the children are used to. But we have been trained to know food values and how one food can take the place of another if necessary ; and we are glad of the opportunity to share that knowledge with you. Here are points from replies to some recent letters.

Your child's milk.
As you know, the allocation is a pint of milk a day for the holder of a Child's Ration Book; half a pint for those who are under eighteen at the end of this year. Not too bad for a nation at war; but not a drop too much. Milk is the most important of all foods for children, _so see that the youngsters get their milk in full._ For instance, a milk pudding made with the children's milk should be eaten only by the children. Make the grown-ups in the family understand that children need milk most.

Dried Peas, beans, oats, national wheatmeal bread, lentils ; each has some body-building nourishment of itself. Combine milk with any one of them, such as in soups, with porridge or as bread and milk and you get not only the added nourishment from the milk, but more body-building value from the other food too. It's as if two and two made five.

For the child who can't or won't drink milk.
Milk will do just as much good in soups, puddings, or cocoa (cocoa adds valuable iron). Some people find milk more digestible, and others like it more, when it is hot, or in cooked dishes.

Something for breakfast.
Something new and delightful, too. Cut some pieces of wheatmeal bread into very small cubes and bake until crisp and golden. Serve hot or cold, with hot or cold milk. This is a good way to use up stale bread or odd crusts. Or make wheatmeal rusks by baking larger pieces or half-slices of wheatmeal bread. Serve them with a drink of milk.

Cheese is good for children.
Cheese is an extremely valuable body-builder and contains material for building bones and teeth. It is therefore a very important food for children. Grate the cheese and sprinkle it on bread or salads, etc. In making cheese dishes, such as macaroni cheese or cheese soups, grate the cheese and add it just at the last moment before serving.

Some foods that give protection against colds.
See that the children get their full ration of butter, margarine and milk. Also plenty of carrots, broccoli tops, watercress, spinach. Mustard and cress, parsley, and tomatoes are very good. So are herrings.

△ The Ministry of Food, in common with the various other ministries, dispensed information and advice and responded to enquiries by means of bulletins in the magazine. The ones shown here date from 1942.

A meaty subject...

Of what use is meat in your diet?
The chief value of meat is to build and repair tissue, but it is only one of the tissue-making foods, and although we must now eat less meat than we like, we can make up for it, from the health point of view, with the others. The most important of these are the animal tissue-builders — milk, cheese, eggs and fish ; then come the vegetable tissue-builders — pulses (dried peas, beans, etc.), oatmeal, national flour and national bread.

Do children need meat?
Children are building their bodies, as well as repairing daily wear and tear. Weight for weight, children need more tissue-builders than grown-ups, and they need more of the animal tissue-builders than the grown-ups. That is why they get a " man-size " ration of meat when they're six, and why they get first call on milk and eggs. Children need their full ration of meat. Never give it to the grown-ups.

She needs as much meat as he does!

Do heavy workers need more meat?
No. Daily wear and tear on the tissues is not materially affected by the kind of work done.

What is the best way to use the meat ration?
Meat should be "stretched" with pulses or oatmeal, etc., and the dish served with greens and potatoes ; then you will get good balanced tissue-building food throughout the week. When pulses are the main part of your dish, add a little chopped meat, bacon, grated cheese or sauce made with milk and you not only get the extra value of the meat, but you enable the vegetables to do you more good. It is as if you added 2 and 2 together and got, not 4, but 5 !

Are some meats better than others?
For practical purposes, all meats are equal. The cheaper cuts are just as nourishing as the dearer, though it may take a little more time and preparation to make them equally appetising. Offals, when you can obtain them, are very good.

RECIPE
1 lb. stewing steak. Root vegetables in season. A breakfastcupful of previously soaked dried peas or beans. Prepare and fry the vegetables in a little fat. Fry the meat on both sides lightly. Cut some of the meat into small pieces, leaving a good-shaped piece of the meat "solid." Place all in a saucepan with the peas or beans, seasoning and water. Simmer gently for about 2 hours. Take out the large piece of meat, and serve the rest as a stew. Part of the main piece of meat can be served cold and the rest sliced and warmed up with hot gravy for other meals.

ISSUED BY THE
MINISTRY OF FOOD

Keeping fit is national service

TAKE
ENO'S
"FRUIT SALT"
Large family size 3/6
Handy size 2/-
(Inclusive of Tax)

In the Forces
In the Workshops
In the Home

Drink Ovaltine

for Strength
Staying Power
and Good Health

P.578A

OVALTINE TABLETS
An emergency ration for eating

'Ovaltine' Tablets contain the energising and sustaining elements of 'Ovaltine.' Carry an emergency supply in your pocket or handbag   In two sizes 1/3d. and 4d.

Build a Better Health

△ By showing women in uniform, advertisers hoped to reinforce the message that it was everyone's duty to stay healthy.

▷ A *Good Housekeeping* editorial of 1943 encourages readers to get out into the sunshine while they can.

HEALTH and gaiety mean more than a fussed-up home : your resistance to
next winter is more important than putting a polish on the dining-room floor.
Build up your health and your family's, now, for the dark days ahead.
Get out into the sunshine, live there as much as you possibly can.
Some of your daily work must be done indoors, admittedly ;
for that work throw open the windows and let the sunshine come to you.
Other jobs, which normally you would do in the kitchen, can be taken
on to a folding table or trolley conveniently near the door.
Outdoor meals ?   Don't confine them to occasional tea.   Have every meal out of doors, every
day when the weather allows.   Children love the casualness of something-
off-a-tray, when hopeful sparrows provide the décor ; you will appreciate
the simplicity of mugs instead of cups and saucers, one knife, one fork and
one spoon for everybody, and no frills whatever.
Making life sunny, making life easy . . . it may seem an odd way to help win the war.
But remember, your health and your children's are vital to your country ;
they are the cause for which one man, perhaps, is fighting with all his heart.

Babies first, please!

For a great many babies Nestlé's Milk is vital – the only milk they can digest and turn to gain and growth.

Over and over again the first feed of Nestlé's Milk has been the turning point in a delicate baby's life. Thousands of mothers will tell you so.

But today there is not always enough Nestlé's to go round, so greatly has the war increased the demand for milk in all its forms. And now that supplies are short, shouldn't we – the rest of us – leave the grocer's limited stocks of Nestlé's Milk for those anxious mothers who have

difficult babies to feed? But if *you* are one of these anxious mothers, tell your grocer. He will do his best for you, we are su.....

Nestlé's.....

a.....

rr.....

vi.....

all.....

pre.....

has.....

Issued by Nestlé's Milk Pro....

CHILD FEEDING IN WARTIME

THAT is the title of the latest GOOD HOUSEKEEPING book, which mothers will find one of the most helpful and timely we have ever produced. It covers the periods 9—12 months, 12—18 months, 18—24 months, and 2—5 years, giving for each age a week's specimen menus, as well as recipes and notes. In addition there are chapters on "Nursery Ways with Milk" and "Principal Food Sources of the Vitamins."

Price 6d., or 7½d. post free from GOOD HOUSEKEEPING, 28-30 Grosvenor Gardens, London, S.W.i.

Look After Yourself

△ Ensuring that babies were adequately and correctly fed during the war was an issue addressed by *Good Housekeeping*, as well as food manufacturers.

▷ A Ministry of Food bulletin from 1943 teaches readers the benefit of vitamins – vital in the days of rationing.

IT'S EASY AS

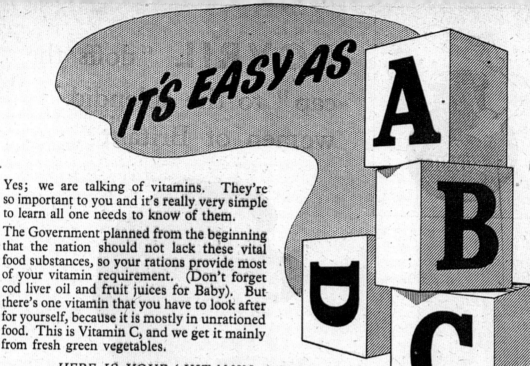

Yes; we are talking of vitamins. They're so important to you and it's really very simple to learn all one needs to know of them.

The Government planned from the beginning that the nation should not lack these vital food substances, so your rations provide most of your vitamin requirement. (Don't forget cod liver oil and fruit juices for Baby). But there's one vitamin that you have to look after for yourself, because it is mostly in unrationed food. This is Vitamin C, and we get it mainly from fresh green vegetables.

HERE IS YOUR 'VITAMIN A B C.'
Why not give it a few minutes' thought, then cut it out and keep it for reference :—

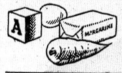

Vitamin A helps to keep healthy the lining of nose, throat and lungs and to lessen liability to colds. Also keeps certain tissues of the eyes in good trim.

Main sources : Your rations of butter and margarine. Also fish liver oil. Dried or fresh eggs. Carrots; green vegetables. Milk.

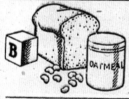

Vitamin B. The vitamins popularly known as B1 and B2 cover many substances, but it is not necessary to learn the complicated details. Together they promote sound digestive systems, steady nerves, prevent fatigue.

Main sources of B1 and B2 : National bread and flour. Dried or fresh eggs. Dried peas and beans. Oatmeal. Bacon. Milk.

Vitamin C gives clear skin, fresh complexion, good teeth. Does much towards establishing general good health and buoyant vitality.

Main sources : Parsley, brussels sprouts, spinach, cabbage, watercress, cauliflower. Rose-hips, blackcurrants, orange juice.

Vitamin C is lessened by cooking; destroyed by long cooking or re-heating. So besides two or three tablespoonfuls daily of lightly cooked green vegetable, eat a good helping of mixed salad — " something green and raw every day." Swedes and turnips are good sources of Vitamin C. Freshly cooked jacket potatoes are very useful. You need three or four of these every day, besides having left-overs fried for breakfast and in made-up dishes, to make up your quota of " at least 1 lb. of potatoes per head per day."

Vitamin D needed for strong bones and sound teeth. Helps to keep chilblains away !

Main sources : Your ration of butter and margarine. Fish liver oil. Herrings and other oily fish. Dried or fresh eggs. Milk.

---

* *Take full advantage of the nation's Immunisation services.*

Protect
your Child

Teach
children
KERB DRILL

See that they always do it
and set a good example by
doing it yourself.

1. At the kerb **HALT**
2. **EYES RIGHT**
3. **EYES LEFT**
   then if the road is clear.
4. **QUICK MARCH**
   Don't rush
   Cross in an orderly manner

3.

◁ ▷ In December 1941 a vitamin welfare scheme for children under two was introduced and they were supplied with free cod liver oil and fruit juice. After the blackout started in September 1939, the lack of streetlights resulted in a huge increase in road accidents, with many children killed and injured.
▽ Between 1940 and 1945 nearly seven million children were vaccinated free of charge against diphtheria.

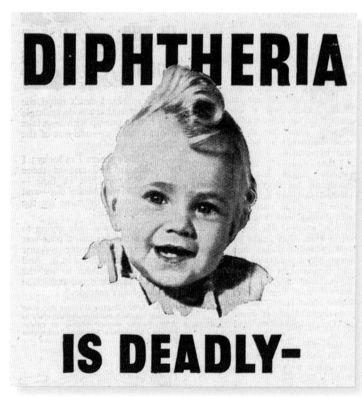

DIPHTHERIA

IS DEADLY-

To Every Mother of an under-6

The Radio Doctor answers questions vital to your children's welfare

Q. I hear a lot about rickets. How can I prevent my unborn baby from having this disease?

A. With cod-liver oil available for every expectant mother and young child in the country there shouldn't be a single case of rickets. Expectant mothers need the Vitamin D contained in cod-liver oil because they are at work on a new human body, the body of the child. Get fish-liver oil tablets — they're easily swallowed — from your clinic or welfare centre. Give the baby a daily dose of cod-liver oil until he is at least five years old. Children need fish-liver oil because Vitamin D is the mortar with which the human bony bricks are held together. Nations are born out of nurseries. And children are like houses. If they are jerry-built they stay that way for life.

Q. Why should my four-year-old need orange juice and cod-liver oil when he is not constipated and looks strong and healthy? I never was one for giving a lot of medicines.

A. These vitamins are not medicines but foods. No matter how flourishing he looks, your child needs the Vitamin D in cod-liver oil to build strong bones, and the Vitamin C in orange juice to protect his good health.

Q. The orange juice seemed to upset my baby when I gave it to her, and my three-year-old refuses to take his cod-liver oil.

A. When you give orange juice to a baby for the first time add plenty of water to the orange juice and a little sugar. Gradually decrease the amount of water. Don't add the juice to his milk.

In the same way start baby on a very small quantity of cod-liver oil, increasing the amount to the full dose when he is accustomed to it. If older children dislike cod-liver oil, give it to them in the form of salad dressing, fish sauce, or with mashed potato. There are plenty of dishes in which it can be mixed without being tasted.

Q. I gave my baby orange juice and cod-liver oil until he was two years old, but is it really necessary for him to have it now? The nearest distributing centre is some distance from my home and I have plenty to do.

A. Your child should have his vitamins for just as long as he has his green ration book. His health may suffer if you stop them now. I know it's an effort to keep that regular date with the centre but it's part of your job as a mother. The Government is doing its part in protecting your child's health by *providing* these vitamin foods. Do your part by seeing that he *gets* them.

HOW TO GET YOUR VITAMIN FOODS

1 Coupons for vitamin foods are now included in the new R.B.2 ration book. If you are an expectant mother you will have an R.B.2 ration book as well — if you have not got it you should get it from the Food Office. You must present a medical certificate when you apply.

2 You can get orange juice and cod-liver oil from any welfare centre, clinic or distributing centre. You need not go to the same one each time.

3 If you are entitled to free milk you will also get free vitamins, but you must apply at the Food Office for " free " coupons. Otherwise each bottle of orange juice costs 5d. and each bottle of cod-liver oil costs 10d. Get 5d. or 10d. stamps or the equivalent in 2½d. stamps from the Post Office and stick them on to the proper coupons. *Produce the stamped coupons in your ration book* at the centre and you will get your own or your child's supplies.

4 For expectant mothers, specially prepared fish-liver oil tablets which are easily swallowed are now available at all distributing centres. Take one each day. The price is 10d. for 45. You can use your cod-liver oil coupons to obtain your supplies.

ISSUED BY THE MINISTRY OF FOOD

To be published this Christmas—

T HIS indomitable little Scottie and Helga, the Norwegian doll, designed by Ethel Ross, can both be made from piece-bag scraps, by means of our paper pattern G.H. Toy No. 4, price 1s. 4d. post free, from Good Housekeeping Needlework Dept., 30 Grosvenor Gardens, London, S.W.1. Helga is 13 in. high, and the dog 6½ in. long. *P.S.*—The Scottie may be purely decorative, with miniature golf clubs in his bag, or may serve a useful purpose by holding spills.

E VERY family their own book publishers—this Christmas when rag-books are unobtainable. We suggest the young artist members of the family work out the designs as simply as possible and in whatever colour schemes the rag-bag materials suggest. Then the needleworkers take over and stitch the pieces in place, adding details, such as eyes, etc., with coloured threads. Next the bookbinders bind the pages together and " publish " in time to find a place on the family Christmas tree.

If the " pages " are of thick material (and every page can be a different colour), the designs are best worked in thin materials. But if you use thin materials for the pages, these should be doubled, as real rag-books used to be.

Try your ideas first with coloured paper pasted in a paper book (which, of course, is an alternative method of production).

We are sure children can think of lots more ideas than those suggested here and on the next page. Very simple, large designs are the easiest to sew in place.

For the Kids

Illustrated by Tage Werner

◁ △ With toys in short supply, the *Good Housekeeping* Needlework
Department offered patterns and suggestions for home-made toys, such
as these from 1944. Other articles advised mothers to interest their children
in indoor gardening, music and painting as outlets for their energies.

Pad those
shoulders well

Wear gored skirts,
placket in front

Be neat and trim—
with a squared cut
smock and slim skirt

A small, soft
pillow helps

those changing

ARE you expecting a small addition to your family? Here are some suggestions to help you to look well and feel well during the months of waiting, without incurring a lot of expense.

Buy two smocks, each a size larger than usual, and pleated —they hang more becomingly. Then pad the shoulders and bust well. Don't be squeamish about discreetly upholstering your top. Choose a plain, but not dismal, colour and if you prefer flowered patterns, have one with a dark background.

Take one of your old gored skirts and wear it with the placket in front. At the waist sew a loop of tape to hook into the fastening at the waistband, leaving the ends to let out as your measurements increase. In this way you will find the skirt gives the appearance of hanging from a slim waist.

Take particular care with your make-up and grooming. Wear a decorative hat, gay scarf or small colourful

Sound Advice

Carry on — as usual

Step out — stride,
don't paddle — in
low-heeled shoes

Wear a pretty hat,
gay scarf, big bag

Curves

brooch, and carry a large handbag at waist level. Wear your clothes with assurance and poise. As with your smocks, keep the shoulders of your swagger coat well padded and wear low-heeled shoes. In other words, fuss about your top and people will forget your girth.

Unless advised by your doctor, don't wear a maternity corset. If you need support, get two 3-in. crêpe bandages and bind yourself with them, not tightly but evenly and comfortably. In the last stages, bind them sling fashion to help to keep the weight off your pelvis. Get a 2-in. wide elastic belt to wear over the hips and fasten your suspenders to this.

In bed at night a small soft cushion under your side often helps you to relax. Wear a brassière at night as well as during the day. Rest, but not too much; live a normal life, take enough exercise—brisk walks are excellent—and the time will fly past.

Rest — but
not too much

△ For expectant mothers *Good Housekeeping* offers sensible and easy-to-follow advice on making a few clothes and accessories last during pregnancy.

'Nobody's Children'

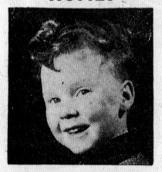
△ Many children were orphaned, abandoned or born out of wedlock during the war. By 1944 almost one baby in three was born illegitimately.

▷ When *Good Housekeeping* ran an article early in 1945 on the plight of unwanted children, it drew a large response.

"Your article 'NOBODY' has disturbed and dis

Passages from readers' letters, showing the interest roused by "Nobody's Children"

" We have thought a lot about your article 'Nobody's Children,' and realise it is not a task to be undertaken lightly. We would like to do something to help to bring a little happiness into the lives of children who are unfortunately in Institutions. We would be willing to answer any questions about ourselves, as we expect references will be necessary."

" . . . We are only ordinary folk, but would take the responsibilities of uncle and aunt seriously. We have two children, a boy 3½ years, and a new baby girl, but we have plenty of room in our hearts for any nephew or niece that might like to adopt us. The idea of writing regularly, a Christmas and birthday gift, is fine, and may I suggest that perhaps a holiday would be allowed when the aunt or uncle took theirs."

" My husband and I have legally adopted four children, and until the wa were all very happy together. Now h is missing (Lieut., Royal Navy), m eldest boy is working away from hom and the girl training in an L.C.C Nursery. The ten-year-old twins ar in boarding-school, and spend thei holidays with me. I am junior mistres in a boys' school, as I must supplemen my government allowance. I shoul dearly like to do something for 'nobody' children.' I have brought up my own family, am a trained teacher and reall fond of children. Please tell me an way in which I can help."

CHILDREN' in the December 'Good Housekeeping'
tressed me beyond words . . . . . ."

My husband and I, alas !, have no children, though we have longed for them, and I feel I would be doing something for those I never had if I could hear more about your idea of becoming an aunt or godparent to one or two of these poor little waifs. . . . At my age (45) there are (one imagines) quite a number of years in which one could help these future fathers and mothers to become good citizens of what is known to be the fairest and most humane-minded nation, and therefore it would be wicked to stand on one side and say ' Let someone else do something, I can't ! "

" The fact that some of the emotion engendered by reading the article remains after the lapse of a fortnight encourages me to think I might make a successful ' uncle.' I realise it is a responsibility not to be lightly undertaken, and I am naturally a bit afraid of myself. However, my wife and I (we have a family of one—a boy, now twelve months old) are interested. Will you please write to us?

" I agree with you that there has been too much thinking and feeling about the plight of these little people, and too little action. Emotion is worse than useless unless it is translated into action."

" So much is said about help—this is the first time I've heard about doing anything, and I should be delighted to get into touch with some little one, boy or girl doesn't matter, who might be willing to take me on as an auntie. I am already regarded as such by the eight children of an old friend of mine in New Zealand, so I think I am suitably qualified ! "

" I should only be too delighted to help some little child who is alone in the world, and try to make up a bit for all the happiness of home life he has missed."

" Your article draws attention to a need which can probably never be met by organised charity, and one which I am sure will find a ready response from all who love children. . . . I have myself three children and understand something of their needs. When this war is over I shall hope to have the time and the means to do something on a larger scale to brighten the lives of a few of these children who miss the joys of home life. Meanwhile, I should like to begin in a small way now by studying the problem and experimenting by the ' adoption ' of two or three children in the restricted sense suggested in your article."

" We have a little boy of our own; nearly two, who is so happy. I should like to try to bring at least a little of that happiness to some other little child. Please send me further particulars.

" If I may say so, I have never read anything which moved me more profoundly. . . . I live alone with my small son of 2½ years. My husband is an R.A.F. pilot serving overseas. Like most women in my position, the days drag quite a lot, and often I have considered a nursery for Ian and a job for myself. But no, I decided on second thoughts to make my son my war job, but how selfish I often feel ! If I could only take a small part in helping in this plan of yours, I should be very happy."

Why, when there are so many children in Institutions, is it so difficult to adopt a child? This and other adoption problems will be discussed by Louise Morgan next month

Spotlight on Service

W.R.N.S.

"Service" is the privilege of all those who, with stout hearts and smiling faces, have joined the ranks of the W.R.N.S. In maintaining a high standard of efficiency they take an immense pride in their work, their responsibilities and their personal appearance. Care of the teeth, for instance, is all-important. Do you, too, use 'Kolynos,' the protective, cleansing and refreshing tooth paste which is rendering such an essential service to the health of the nation?

IMPORTANT. Don't throw away your empty tube; the Nation needs the metal. Please return it to your local chemist or store when making your next purchase.

KOLYNOS DENTAL CREAM

A SCIENTIFIC DENTAL CREAM

HIGHLY CONCENTRATED ½ INCH IS ENOUGH

CLEANSING REFRESHING ECONOMICAL

The Economical Tooth Paste

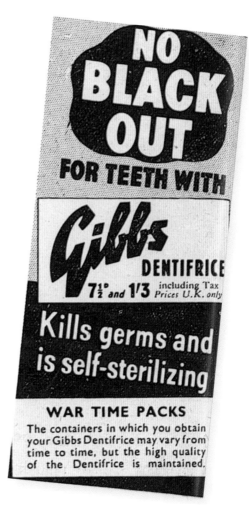

◁ Advertisers regularly employed the theme that by using their product you would be doing a service to the nation, as this one from June 1943 shows.

△ By 1941 toothbrushes and toothpaste tubes were sometimes also in short supply, since metal and plastic were needed for the war effort.

Keep Smiling Through

'Women's Troubles'

"Now She MUST Carry On"

War will not wait on woman's weakness, nor need any woman "go sick" on account of periodic pains and headaches. Just take one or two A-K Tablets and you will be able to carry on as usual.

If you suffer from regular pain you must try A-K Tablets. They cost so little and bring such comfort that you owe it to yourself. They relieve pain in a few minutes and their effect is lasting. Join the thousands of women who have found A-K a safe, sure method of relieving periodic pain. Don't suffer another month. Get A-K Tablets to-day, and enjoy this freedom from pain.

NOTE.—A-K is how thousands of women ask for *Anti-Kamnia* brand Analgesic Tablets, and if you say A-K your chemist will know. 1/5 a box (including Tax).

Things have changed since Grandma's days

Then, women just had to put up with many things which nowadays would not be tolerated. Knowledge on many vital subjects was limited —women expected to be "in poor health" from 40 onwards. To-day such middle-age suffering need not be, because modern medical science has discovered its cause and also found the remedy. Menopax —a most up-to-date medicine for such troubles—restores the equilibrium of the upset body metabolism—the cause of women's suffering at this time of life.

MENOPAX
for Women's Middle-age Suffering

Prices 2/10, 5/7½ and 11/3 from Boots, Timothy Whites, Taylors and all leading chemists. An interesting book, "The Crisis in a Woman's Life," may be taken FREE from most chemists' counters, or sent direct for 3d. in stamps by:

CLINICAL PRODUCTS Lᵗᴰ
2, THE GREEN, RICHMOND, SURREY

△ For women doing men's jobs in the war, weakness was frowned upon, as this advertisement from 1940 shows, while in 1942 Menopax shies away from explicit explanations.
▷ In 1941 Tampax took advantage of women's roles in the war to show them as liberated users of their product.

WOMEN of the services

are winning the war of *freedom*

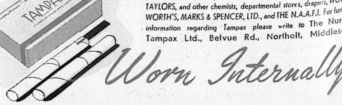

Ten plain facts about

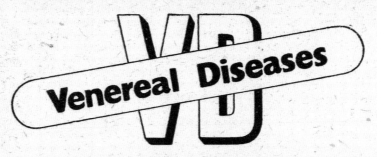

Venereal Diseases

"It is very important under present conditions that the public should know of the existence of venereal diseases; their prevalence in war-time; how they are caused; the urgent necessity for early treatment; and where advice and treatment can be obtained."—THE MINISTER OF HEALTH.

1. Venereal Diseases have increased since the war and are still increasing; 70,000 new cases are now occurring yearly among civilians alone. Venereal diseases cause much misery. They bring tragedy into many homes, and considerably damage our war effort by causing reduced efficiency and wasted hours.

2. Ignorance and secrecy are highly dangerous. Only from a plain and frank statement of the facts can we all know what these diseases are, how they are spread, how they can be avoided and how and where they can be cured.

3. The two principal venereal diseases are syphilis and gonorrhœa. They are caused by quite different living organisms or germs.

4. Syphilis is a dangerous, a killing disease. If not treated early and thoroughly by a doctor it can cause serious mutilation, heart disease, paralysis, and insanity. Syphilis can be passed on to an unborn child from its mother and (unless skilled treatment is given early in pregnancy) is one of the causes of blindness, deafness, and mental defects.

5. Gonorrhœa, though not so dangerous to life, is more serious than is generally believed, and is one of the causes of arthritis, sterility and chronic ill-health.

6. Syphilis and gonorrhœa are almost always contracted through intercourse with an infected person. The germs of these diseases quickly die outside the human body. In practice, therefore, there is no need to fear their spread by accidental infection.

7. Professional prostitutes are not the only source of infection. Any free-and-easy sex behaviour must mean a risk of infection and cannot be made safe. Clean living is the only way to escape infection—abstinence is not harmful.

8. Venereal diseases can be cured if treated *early* by a specialist doctor. Advice and treatment are available at the clinics set up by County and County Borough Councils for the purpose. Treatment is free, confidential and *effective*. Any family doctor or Medical Officer of Health will give the address of the nearest clinic. Quack treatment or self-treatment is absolutely useless and may even be disastrous.

9. Disappearance of the early symptoms does not necessarily mean that the patient has been cured. It is essential to continue the treatment until the doctor says it may be stopped.

10. Anyone who has the slightest reason to suspect infection should seek medical treatment AT ONCE. A doctor or clinic should be consulted immediately about any suspicious sore or unusual discharge. It may not be venereal disease, but it is best to be sure.

These are the signs. The first sign of syphilis is a small ulcer. It appears from 10 to 90 days after infection; usually about three weeks.

Gonorrhœa first shows itself as a discharge which usually appears from 2 to 10 days after infection.

Further information can be obtained IN CONFIDENCE from the local Health Department, or from the Medical Adviser, Central Council for Health Education, Tavistock House, Tavistock Square, London, W.C.1 (Phone: Euston 3341).

ISSUED BY THE MINISTRY OF HEALTH AND THE CENTRAL COUNCIL FOR HEALTH EDUCATION

(V.D.1-4)

* Spend less on yourself—Lend more to your country.

TO ALL THINKING WOMEN

ON the opposite page we publish an advertisement from the Ministry of Health on the subject of venereal diseases. For a family magazine this may seem, at first sight, a strange step. But just because GOOD HOUSEKEEPING is edited for, and by, those who believe whole-heartedly in the sanctity of the home; who believe that, above all, our children's heritage must be safeguarded and this country, and the world, made a better, cleaner, saner place to live in, it is only logical that it should draw attention to an evil menacing all we hold dear.

Here, too, we want to make one point. Much danger lies in the fact that the ordinary decent citizen, especially when a woman, feels that "V.D." is so remote from her life and home that, though to be deplored, it is not really her concern. How tragic a fallacy this is appears every day.

A clean, intelligent lad, son of whom any mother may be proud, joins up. Away from home and friends, eager for fun and companionship in his off-duty hours, an evening that starts innocently enough may end up disastrously. The fact that a boy would not seek the company of prostitutes does not mean safety. An appalling number of venereal infections are caused by quite young girls who seem, on the surface, perfectly fit companions for decent lads.

Not always, of course, is it the boys who suffer most. Many a young married couple have had their happiness blasted because the husband, before marriage, and as the price, perhaps, of a single escapade, contracted a venereal infection and then, not fully cured, passed it on to his wife and unborn child.

No, not one of us can say "this cannot touch me or mine": all of us have the duty to do whatever lies in our power to stamp out the scourge.

What can we women do? First and foremost, perhaps, make our home life so warm and full and rich that husbands, sons, daughters, wherever they may be, even if miles away, will feel its call stronger and more compelling than any temptation.

Next, too, those of us who are blessed in our own home lives can lend a helping hand to the less well-placed. If the young men and girls in the Services, or working in factories away from home, had more of the right kind of hospitality offered them, more pleasant, friendly places where both sexes could enjoy each other's company, there would be far less dangerous playing with fire.

The aim of all thinking women must be to obviate the conditions—loneliness, a feeling of insecurity and not being wanted, with the resultant craving for excitement and attention—that so often lead to sexual promiscuity. If, however, damage has been done, swift and specialised medical attention is imperative. In such cases, an understanding older woman can do much to persuade the sufferer to take treatment at once. The toll of V.D. must be arrested, and it is we wives and mothers who can do much to help.

Pulling no Punches

◁ △ The Ministry of Health's campaign in 1942 on the subject of VD highlighted the huge increase in the spread of the disease since war had begun.

▷ Ads such as this one pulled no punches to get their message across.

Death to Vermin

Consolidating the Bridgehead of Rat Control

In planning an invasion, if success so far as humanly possible is to be assured—careful consideration must be given to the tactical defence and consolidation of bridgeheads.

The problem applies equally in the war against rats and mice: and the successful clearance of infested areas depends upon the care and forethought given to the defensive—as well as the offensive—measures taken once a bridgehead is established.

This fact is fully appreciated by the skilful surveyors of the Ratin Company, who, in conjunction with the Company's scientists have perfected a plan of campaign which embraces not only a proven formula for the destruction of rodents, but also a plan of consolidation for those premises cleared of the pest. Thus, premises brought under control by the Ratin method are under skilled observation at carefully regulated intervals to ensure that they are not re-infested by a sudden counter-attack.

It is upon the thoroughness and integrity of its surveyors and operators as much as on the Company's scientists, that the success of the Ratin method depends, and the ever-increasing number of public and prominent private undertakings employing the Ratin Service is an irrefutable testimony to the work of national importance which they are performing.

THE BRITISH RATIN CO LTD

125 PALL MALL LONDON S.W.1
Telephone: ABBey 7621

◁ Bomb damage throughout the country led to rodents in the ruins. This ad from 1943 suggests a battle plan against their invasion.
▷ The nation's food at risk - the message implicit in these ads was that it was your national duty to take action.

Steam Flies attacking nation's food reserves

Serious damage to stored food-stuffs—particularly flour, cereals, meals and dried fruit—is being caused by Steam Flies (or, to give them their scientific name, Blattella Germanica, of the Cockroach group).

The Steam Fly, which infests hotels, restaurants, canteens, bakeries, hospitals, and centrally-heated buildings, where it swarms in incredible numbers, is a prolific breeder—it is recorded that forty young flies were produced from a single egg-pouch.

The loss of prestige and goodwill to firms supplying products contaminated by Steam Flies is only outweighed, and that to a serious extent, by the loss to the nation of valuable food supplies.

The Pest-Control Service operated by Chelsea Insecticides, Ltd., has made a special study of the problem of the Steam Fly; and also effectively deals with infestations of beetles, cockroaches and crickets.

Illustrations show adult Steam Fly and oötheca. The slightest suspicion of either on your premises is the signal to communicate with Chelsea Insecticides, Ltd., at once.

CHELSEA INSECTICIDES *Service*

WARTIME
Food & Recipes

In autumn 1939 ration books were issued and in
January 1940, shortly after the war had begun,
food rationing was introduced. Initially, sugar,
bacon and butter were rationed, but over the
course of the new few months meat, tea,
margarine and other fats joined the list. Canned
food became a staple of many diets until it, too,
was rationed in November 1941 and by 1942
most foodstuffs were rationed to some extent.
Bread, alcohol and cigarettes, however, although
in short supply, were available without coupons.

At the outbreak of the war, with the prospect of
food in short supply, people were urged to grow
their own and the Dig for Victory campaign was
introduced. *Good Housekeeping* published articles
on gardening, preserving, salting, drying and
bottling and the nation got digging, while the
Good Housekeeping Institute showed readers how
to make nutritious meals from their rations and
feed the family on £3.10s a week.

WONDERFUL AIDS
FOR YOUR WAR-TIME COOKING

A delicious **VANILLA FLAVOURING** for all cooking purposes. This is highly concentrated and should be used sparingly. 7½ D.

Imparts that delicate nutty flavour of **ALMONDS** Use sparingly. 6 D.

Also Ground Almond Substitute sold in bulk.

ASHEX EGG SUBSTITUTE will do everything an egg will do except boil or fry. Doubles the quantity of your scrambled eggs.

SIZES 2 D. & 9 D.

OR-EX Orange Flavour may be used for cooking, orange drinks and cocktails. 7½ D.

LEM-EX Ashex Lemon Flavour can be used for all cooking purposes, and added to water will make a delicious lemon drink. 6 D.

SOLD BY ALL GROCERS

MANUFACTURED BY **ASHE LABORATORIES LTD** 120/122 VICTORIA ST. LONDON S.W.1

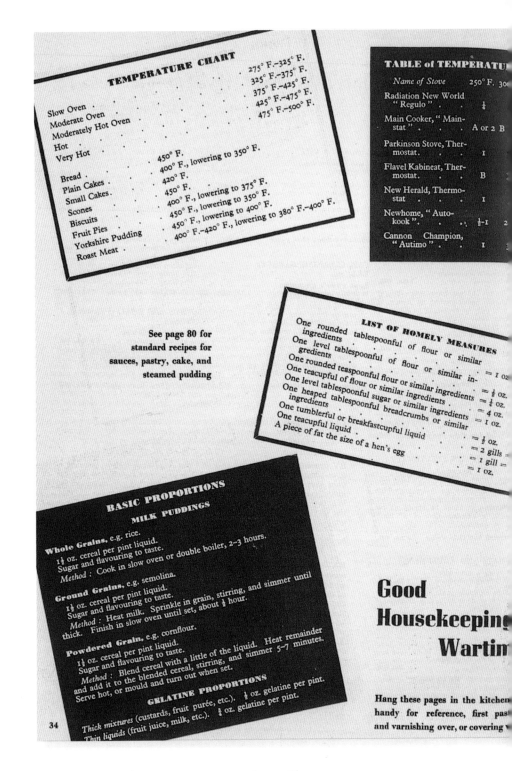

TEMPERATURE CHART

Slow Oven	275° F.–325° F.
Moderate Oven	325° F.–375° F.
Moderately Hot Oven	375° F.–425° F.
Hot	425° F.–475° F.
Very Hot	475° F.–500° F.

Bread	450° F.
Plain Cakes	400° F., lowering to 350° F.
Small Cakes	420° F.
Scones	450° F.
Biscuits	400° F., lowering to 375° F.
Fruit Pies	450° F., lowering to 350° F.
Yorkshire Pudding	450° F., lowering to 400° F.
Roast Meat	450° F., lowering to 380° F.–400° F.
	400° F.–420° F., lowering to 380° F.–400° F.

TABLE of TEMPERATU

Name of Stove	250° F.	30
Radiation New World "Regulo"	¼	
Main Cooker, "Main-stat"	A or 2 B	
Parkinson Stove, Ther-mostat.	1	
Flavel Kabineat, Ther-mostat.	B	
New Herald, Thermo-stat	1	
Newhome, "Auto-kook".	½–1	2
Cannon Champion, "Autimo".	1	2

See page 80 for
standard recipes for
sauces, pastry, cake, and
steamed pudding

LIST OF HOMELY MEASURES

One rounded tablespoonful of flour or similar ingredients	= 1 oz
One level tablespoonful of flour or similar ingredients	
One rounded teaspoonful flour or similar ingredients	= ½ oz.
One teacupful of flour or similar ingredients	= ¼ oz.
One level tablespoonful sugar or similar ingredients	= 4 oz.
One heaped tablespoonful breadcrumbs or similar ingredients	= 1 oz.
One tumblerful or breakfastcupful liquid	= ½ oz.
One teacupful liquid	= 2 gills =
A piece of fat the size of a hen's egg	= 1 gill =
	= 1 oz.

BASIC PROPORTIONS

MILK PUDDINGS

Whole Grains, e.g. rice.
1½ oz. cereal per pint liquid.
Sugar and flavouring to taste.
Method : Cook in slow oven or double boiler, 2–3 hours.

Ground Grain, e.g. semolina.
1½ oz. cereal per pint liquid.
Sugar and flavouring to taste.
Method : Heat milk. Sprinkle in grain, stirring, and simmer until thick. Finish in slow oven until set, about ½ hour.

Powdered Grain, e.g. cornflour.
1½ oz. cereal per pint liquid.
Sugar and flavouring to taste.
Method : Blend cereal with a little of the liquid. Heat remainder and add it to the blended cereal, stirring, and simmer 5–7 minutes.
Serve hot, or mould and turn out when set.

GELATINE PROPORTIONS

Thick mixtures (custards, fruit purée, etc.). ¼ oz. gelatine per pint.
Thin liquids (fruit juice, milk, etc.). ⅜ oz. gelatine per pint.

34

**Good
Housekeeping
Wartim**

Hang these pages in the kitchen
handy for reference, first pas
and varnishing over, or covering

Cooking Advice

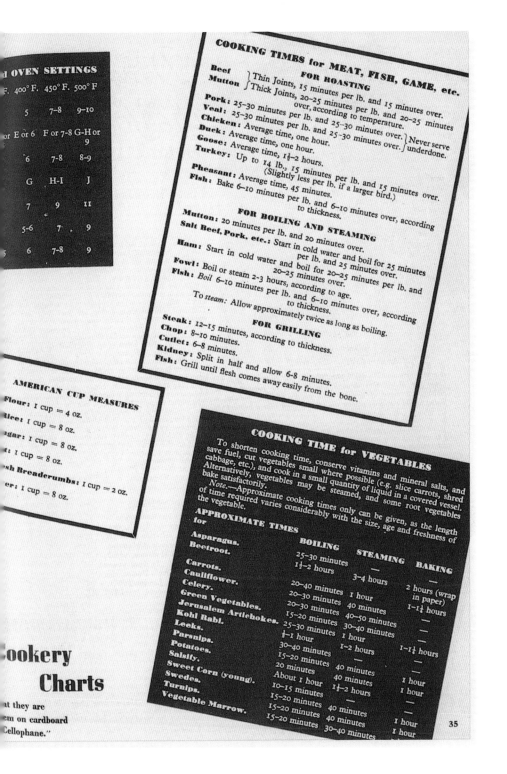

F.	400° F.	450° F.	500° F
	5	7-8	9-10
or E or 6	F or 7-8	G-H or 9	
6	7-8	8-9	
G	H-I	J	
7	9	11	
5-6	7	9	
6	7-8	9	

COOKING TIMES for MEAT, FISH, GAME, etc.

FOR ROASTING

Beef
Mutton } Thin Joints, 15 minutes per lb. and 15 minutes over.
Thick Joints, 20-25 minutes per lb. and 20-25 minutes over, according to temperature.

Pork: 25-30 minutes per lb. and 25-30 minutes over. } Never serve
Veal: 25-30 minutes per lb. and 25-30 minutes over. } underdone.

Chicken: Average time, one hour.
Duck: Average time, one hour.
Goose: Average time, 1½-2 hours.
Turkey: Up to 14 lb., 15 minutes per lb. and 15 minutes over.
(Slightly less per lb. if a larger bird.)
Pheasant: Average time, 45 minutes.
Fish: Bake 6-10 minutes per lb. and 6-10 minutes over, according to thickness.

FOR BOILING AND STEAMING

Mutton: 20 minutes per lb. and 20 minutes over.
Salt Beef, Pork, etc.: Start in cold water and boil for 25 minutes per lb. and 25 minutes over.
Ham: Start in cold water and boil for 20-25 minutes per lb. and 20-25 minutes over.
Fowl: Boil or steam 2-3 hours, according to age.
Fish: Boil 6-10 minutes per lb. and 6-10 minutes over, according to thickness.

To *steam:* Allow approximately twice as long as boiling.

FOR GRILLING

Steak: 12-15 minutes, according to thickness.
Chop: 8-10 minutes.
Cutlet: 6-8 minutes.
Kidney: Split in half and allow 6-8 minutes.
Fish: Grill until flesh comes away easily from the bone.

AMERICAN CUP MEASURES

Flour: 1 cup = 4 oz.
[R]ice: 1 cup = 8 oz.
[Su]gar: 1 cup = 8 oz.
[Fa]t: 1 cup = 8 oz.
[Fre]sh Breadcrumbs: 1 cup = 2 oz.
[Butt]er: 1 cup = 8 oz.

[C]ookery Charts

[...]t they are
[...]m on cardboard
[...]Cellophane."

COOKING TIME for VEGETABLES

To shorten cooking time, conserve vitamins and mineral salts, and save fuel, cut vegetables small where possible (e.g. slice carrots, shred cabbage, etc.), and cook in a small quantity of liquid in a covered vessel. Alternatively, vegetables may be steamed, and some root vegetables bake satisfactorily.

Note.—Approximate cooking times only can be given, as the length of time required varies considerably with the size, age and freshness of the vegetable.

APPROXIMATE TIMES

for	BOILING	STEAMING	BAKING
Asparagus.	25-30 minutes	—	
Beetroot.	1½-2 hours	3-4 hours	2 hours (wrap in paper)
Carrots.	20-40 minutes	1 hour	1-1½ hours
Cauliflower.	20-30 minutes	40 minutes	
Celery.	20-30 minutes	40-50 minutes	
Green Vegetables.	15-20 minutes	40-50 minutes	
Jerusalem Artichokes.	25-30 minutes	30-40 minutes	
Kohl Rabi.	½-1 hour	1 hour	
Leeks.	30-40 minutes	1-2 hours	1-1½ hours
Parsnips.	15-20 minutes		
Potatoes.	20 minutes	40 minutes	
Salsify.	About 1 hour	40 minutes	1 hour
Sweet Corn (young).	10-15 minutes	1½-2 hours	1 hour
Swedes.	15-20 minutes		
Turnips.	15-20 minutes	40 minutes	1 hour
Vegetable Marrow.	15-20 minutes	40 minutes	1 hour
	30-40 minutes		

35

△ The Good Housekeeping Institute today might not endorse this advice, given in January 1942, to boil asparagus for 25-30 minutes!

△ This map from 1942 was designed to illustrate the risks and difficulties confronting those responsible for replenishing the nation's stocks of food, and why the population could expect to receive only those things that were really needed.

A Small World

Dig For Victory

I was front-page news a year ago . . . . the rarest and most discussed of all foods. And why? Simply because you relied upon having me brought from abroad. Women are wiser now! They and the older children are "Digging for Victory"—GROWING THEIR OWN onions and other vegetables to ensure their family supplies the whole year round. Are *you* digging yet? For remember, the garden or allotment is also your job now. So start to-day, and have all the vegetables you want next season—without paying or queuing for them!

YOU SEE, I AM ONE OF THOSE CROPS YOU CAN STORE

DIG FOR VICTORY NOW!

POST THIS COUPON NOW (Unsealed envelope, 1d. stamp)

TO MINISTRY OF AGRICULTURE, HOTEL LINDUM, ST. ANNES-ON-SEA, LANCS.
Please send copies of free pictorial leaflets, 'How to Dig' & 'How to Crop'.

NAME ....

ADDRESS ....

A.99

ISSUED BY THE MINISTRY OF AGRICULTURE

◁ Once the war began, the nation got digging and sowing to provide vegetables and fruit to supplement the meagre rations, and by 1943 nearly 1½ million allotments were being cultivated. ▷ These advertisements from 1942 and 1943 suggest ways in which readers can use their home-grown produce, while *Good Housekeeping* offered seeds for growing unusual vegetables.

HERE'S A PRETTY PICKLE!

Garden vegetables make delicious and piquant pickles. Fruit from the garden makes excellent chutney — spicy or sweet as you prefer. Write for Cookery Notes No. 31, approved by the Ministry of Food—it is full of new, tested recipes for pickles, chutneys and home-made sauces that will last the year round.

STORK MARGARINE COOKERY SERVICE

Send this today

...coupon to The Stork
...Uni-

Please send me a copy of Cookery Notes No. 31 " Pickles from Garden Vegetables."

Name ....

Street ....

Town ....

SOW... GROW...
AND THEN ADD OXO

MIXED VEGETABLE FLA...

(Enough for 4)

½ oz dripping
½ pt. vegetable water
1 tablespoon grated cheese
½ oz. flour
1 lb. mixed cooked vegetables
Parsley to garnish
Oxo Cube

Line a flan tin with short pastry. Cook about 15 minutes in a very hot oven, Regulo No. 7. Meanwhile melt the dripping in a pan and stir in the flour. Dissolve the Oxo cube in vegetable water and add it gradually. Stir until thick. Add the cut-up vegetables. Make really hot. Turn into the cooked flan case. Sprinkle with the cheese and garnish with parsley. Serve hot.

LET **OXO** MEAT YOUR VEGETABLES

WOMEN!
Farmers can't grow all your vegetables

BROCCOLI
POTATOES
CABBAGE
WHEAT
ONIONS
FODDER FOR DAIRY COWS
BRUSSELS SPROUTS
BARLEY for BREAD

YOU MUST GROW YOUR OWN

Farmers are growing more of the other essential crops—potatoes, corn for your bread and food for the cows. It's up to *you* to provide the vegetables that are vital to your children's health —especially in winter. Grow all you can. If you don't, they may go short. Turn your garden over to vegetables. Get the older children to help you. If you haven't a garden ask your local council for an allotment. DO IT NOW.

DIG
for Victory

ISSUED BY THE MINISTRY OF AGRICULTURE

While the men are away
Women must DIG

The children *must* have green vegetables for health—particularly in winter. Growing them is now largely a job for women. Don't rely on others—farmers must use their fields for other vital crops.

ACT NOW If you haven't a garden, ask your local council for an allotment.

PLAN WISELY It's winter vegetables you will need most—cabbages, kale, broccoli, brussels sprouts. By planning your planting you will make sure of getting enough.

THESE FREE ILLUSTRATED LEAFLETS WILL SHOW YOU HOW TO

DIG
Dig for Victory leaflet No. 20.

PLAN
Dig for Victory leaflet No. I.

SOW SEEDS Dig for Victory leaflet No. 19.

Get them from your local council offices or from the Ministry of Agriculture, Hotel Lindum, St. Annes-on-Sea, Lancs.

DIG *for Victory*

ISSUED BY THE MINISTRY OF AGRICULTURE

more important than ever.

WISE housewives will by this time have turned out their bottle cupboards and made a survey of all the available jam jars and bottles. Jars should have been paired up with their lids and screws or clips, rubber bands tested, lacquered lids examined and all necessary replacements made.

If you have not already done this, do it at once. Don't wait until the fruit is on the kitchen table—the fruit won't improve by lying there while you make an expedition to the shops, and you will suffer disappointment if you find, too late, that the supply of " spares " has already given out in your locality.

There is far more about bottling and jam-making than can be told in this small space. The full story is given in *Good Housekeeping Wartime Preserves* (price 9d., or 10½d., including postage), which is both complete guide for the novice and reference book for the experienced.

BOTTLING

A Word about Equipment

Special bottling apparatus is no essential, though a steriliser is ver convenient, of course, and a cannin machine is a delightful luxury. How ever, you do need jars, and some mean of making them airtight. To sterilis them you can use any receptable that i deep enough to allow of the jars bein immersed in the water—or you ca sterilise in the oven.

For the Campden* method, airtigh jars are all that is required. Sterilisin by heat is not necessary when preserving fruit in this solution.

Suitable Jars and Covers

Special bottling jars, fitted wit rubber rings and lids, secured wit screw bands or clips, are the mos convenient and are suitable for al methods of sterilising. Some peopl prefer the clips, since once these are i position they need no further adjust ment. With screw bands you have t remember to loosen the screws slightl before sterilising, to allow air and stean to escape. To ensure a satisfactory seal it is important to screw down ver tightly immediately after sterilising and again after a few minutes' interval

Converting Jam Jars

Special covers of lacquered meta with rubber ring and clip, have been o the market for several seasons, and i

The Ministry of Food asks us again to preserve as much as we can of the produce of the garden to help fill the Nation's larder for the winter months ahead. Good Housekeeping Institute will gladly help you with any difficulties

BOTTLING

* Turn out your rag bag: it may make a glad bag.

Preserve your Food

sed with care these can be very satisfactory. The jars must be of standard size (1 or 2 lb.) and the rims quite perfect, that is to say, not only free from chips and lumps, but also having no ridge inside the rim of the glass where the rubber ring has to make contact with it. The lid needs to be adjusted carefully, and must be held firmly in position by the clip. The clips are pliable and can be bent to a more acute angle, if necessary, to effect this. In time the lacquer on these covers wears off, exposing the metal underneath. When this happens they must be discarded, as they cannot be relacquered at home.

New this season is another

the packets and should be followed carefully.

The synthetic skin in sheet form has already been used by many of our readers, who will be glad to hear that the skin being manufactured this year is an improvement on last season's and more like the original version. The particular usefulness of the skin lies in the fact that it can be cut to fit any shape of jar. The manufacturers' directions should be carefully followed when using this synthetic skin with either method of sterilising by heat. When employed with the Campden Solution, the skin is merely tied down tightly over the jars, as heating is not necessary.

edge slightly, another layer of the melted fat should be poured on, so that the seal is perfect.

A Last Resort

Failing all else, a paper-and-paste cover can be quite useful, but it is best not to attempt to store jars covered in this way for a long period. Choose paper that is thin yet strong, and allow 4–5 circles for each jar, large enough to come down as far as the shoulder. Brush these with flour-and-water paste and apply them, one on top of another, to the jar of sterilised fruit, pressing well to make them adhere and smoothing down the creases.

(*Continued on page* 98)

Homely Methods

Paraffin wax or clarified mutton is after all what our grandparents used, though nowadays simple homecraft seems a lost art and many people complain of finding the wax method difficult and unsatisfactory. The important thing is to make sure that the inside of the neck of the bottle is dry and free from fruit juice. Then pour on the melted (but not boiling) fat so gently that it lies on the surface in a layer—about $\frac{1}{4}$ to $\frac{1}{2}$ in. thick. During cooling, when the fat shrinks and draws away from the

method of converting standard 1-lb. jam jars for use in bottling. It consists of a lacquered metal clip-on cover into which is fitted a ring of synthetic skin. Extremely easy to use, this method gives very good results, provided the jar is of standard size and not chipped. Directions for using them are contained in

AM-MAKING

By Jane Creswell

(*Combined Domestic Subjects Diploma, Gloucester*)

* *Start patching and mending instead of spending.*

29

The Ministry of Food has approved this Article

△ The seasonal gluts of home-grown produce inspired the magazine in July 1943 to publish a helpful guide. *Good Housekeeping Wartime Preserves.* while the Women's Institute opened hundreds of preserving centres.

By Jane Creswell (*Combined Domestic Science Diploma, Gloucester*)

DURING the next few months we shall be reaping the fruits of our toil in the garden and allotment, and while we should enjoy the freshness of the young vegetables now being gathered, we should also look ahead to the winter and preserve every scrap of the surplus crop while it is still in its prime.

Bottling and jam-making are not the only ways of preserving garden produce. Drying, pickling and salting are simple processes and should form part of the careful housewife's preserving programme this summer. Here are a few hints which may help you with these processes, though for "step-by-step" instructions you should consult **Good Housekeeping War-time Preserves**, price 9*d.*, or 10½*d.* including postage, from our Centre, at 28/30 Grosvenor Gardens, London, S.W.1.

Drying

Apples, pears, grapes and stone fruit, besides onions and mushrooms, can all be successfully preserved by drying. This method was not much practised in England before the war, since the climate is not ideal for outdoor drying ; but during the last few years we have found that drying by artificial heat can give very good—and very useful—results.

Alternative Methods . . .

A cool oven, a shelf in the airing cupboard, or the heat rising from a boiler or radiator can all be used. The important point is to keep the temperature below 140° F. if possible, but not so low that mould growth will set in.

Spread them out . . .

Put the fruits or vegetables on racks, sieves or muslin-covered wooden frames for drying (or thread on canes or fine string when suitable), so that the air can circulate properly. If trays are used the foodstuffs must be frequently turned.

How to Test . . .

Vegetables and herbs should be dried until crisp. Fruits, such as plums and grapes, do not reach this stage—when ready they are leathery in texture and give no juice when squeezed.

Storage . . .

Store dried fruits and vegetables as you wo currants and raisins—in a store jar, tin or wooden b They should, of course, be covered, but there is necessity to make the container airtight.

Pickling

Pickles and chutneys have always been popu with English people ; since pickles require sugar, and chutneys v little, there is no need for to ration ourselves w home-made preserves this sort. Almost all veg ables can be successfu pickled or made into ch ney. Pickling consists sentially of two processe brining, and the additio vinegar, spiced if possi Chutney is a cooked mixt of vegetables combined w spices, some sugar and v often fruits, both fresh dried. Most recipes chutneys contain a fair p portion of onions or shall which add greatly to flavour.

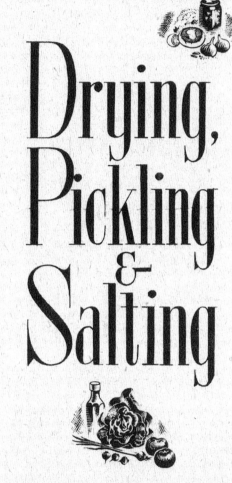

Vinegar for Pickling . . .

It is important that vinegar used should have acetic acid content of less than 6 per cent. you use a reputable bra it will be safe to assu that this percentage present.

Spices if Possible . . .

Recipes for pickles u ally recommend spic vinegar, i.e. vinegar which a mixture of spic has been infused. But sin most spices come fr abroad, you may have manage with fewer this year, or even with none all. Spiced pickles are more interesting in flavo of course, but the spices are by no means essential.

Brining is Essential . . .

This important process should not be omitte Its purpose is to take away some of the exce moisture from the vegetables, and so prevent much dilution of the vinegar. There are t methods of brining—dry brining, i.e. sprinkli with dry salt, for watery vegetables such as cucu ber, marrow or tomatoes ; and wet brining "dry" vegetables, such as cauliflower, onions a shallots. Whichever method is used, the vegeta should be thoroughly rinsed afterwards, or t pickle may taste too salty. (*Continued on page 5*

Drying, Pickling & Salting

Store-house of health

At one time tomatoes were grown purely as decorative novelties, and were known by the charming name of love-apples. Now we know that tomatoes are a grand protective food; that they help to clear the complexion, give buoyant health and vitality, and guard against infection.

Much of the goodness of tomatoes is retained in bottling. So bottle as many as you can, not only for their healthfulness but for the refreshing flavour and attractive colour tomatoes add to your winter meals.

The juice is equally precious, so use every drop, in soups or sauces, and perhaps for some appetising tomato juice cocktails.

Here are a couple of easy methods of bottling tomatoes. Why not do some today? Other simple ways are given in a leaflet—see offer below.

Bottling Tomatoes whole :
OVEN METHOD

JARS. There are several kinds on the market. Also various tops to use with jam jars. If you use jam jars, make sure that the rims are a perfect circle, and that the tops fit. Make sure you get the right size rings, etc. Test before using (fill jars with cold water, put on rubber rings, tops and bands or clips, wipe dry and stand jars head down for half an hour. If they leak, examine for defects ; try another rubber ring, or adjust clip). Rinse and drain jars before use.

METHOD

1. Wash the tomatoes and pack them, whole, into jars, gently but as closely as possible. Fill right to top to allow for shrinkage as they cook.

2. Put them in a slow oven (about 240° F.) and stand them on cardboard or thicknesses of paper to prevent cracking. Cover the group of bottles with a shallow baking-tin or browning sheet whilst the tomatoes are cooking.

3. Sterilise tops and rings (not band or clips) by putting them in cold water, bringing to boil and boiling 15 minutes ; use while hot.

4. When the tomatoes appear cooked (they *must* be cooked for at least 1½ hrs.), and are slightly shrunk, take out one jar at a time ; place on mat or folded paper, pour in boiling brine (½-oz. salt dissolved in 1 qt. water) to overflowing; a little sugar (½-oz.) may be added to the brine before filling bottles, if desired. Seal immediately with hot sterilised rubber rings and top, then band or clip. Screw-bands may need tightening as jar cools. Test next day; take off clip or band, lift jar by lid; if it stays on seal is perfect. If lid comes off, that jar is faulty and must be re-done or used within a few days.

Pulping Tomatoes

Wash, cut up tomatoes, cook in just enough water to prevent pan burning until thoroughly cooked and reduced to pulp. Then sprinkle ¼ teaspoon salt to each 2 lb. tomatoes. Stir well. Meanwhile heat jars in oven and sterilise tops and rings as explained above. Then fill one jar at a time, keeping pulp, jars and rings and tops *hot* during the whole process of bottling. Seal, but give any screw-bands a slight turn backwards to allow for expansion. Place jars in a pan of boiling water so that the boiling water completely covers them. Boil for 10 minutes. Remove, tighten screw-bands, and test next day for "Oven method."

FREE LEAFLET :

"Preservation of Tomatoes"

giving simple directions for bottling tomatoes in their own juice; for bottling in deep pan or sterilizer, etc., gladly sent on request. Please send a p.c. for it to Ministry of Food, Dept. 627E, Food Advice Division, London, W.1.

(S98)   **ISSUED BY THE MINISTRY OF FOOD**

◁ △ Preserving foods for the cold months of winter was the subject of many magazine articles. Anything edible was made use of, not only as food, but as infusions for tea or distilled into alcoholic drinks.

Get Pickling

"DRIED EGGS
are <u>my</u> eggs—
my <u>whole</u> eggs
and
<u>nothing but my eggs</u>"

Dried eggs are the complete hen's eggs, both the white and the yolk, dried to a powder. Nothing is added. Nothing but moisture and the shell taken away, leaving the eggs themselves as wholesome, as digestible and as full of nourishment and health-protecting value as if you had just taken the eggs new laid from the nest. So put the eggs back into your breakfast menus. And what about a big, creamy omelette for supper? You can have it savoury; or sweet, now that you get extra jam.

DRIED EGGS build you up!

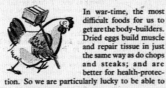

In war-time, the most difficult foods for us to get are the body-builders. Dried eggs build muscle and repair tissue in just the same way as do chops and steaks; and are better for health-protection. So we are particularly lucky to be able to get dried eggs to make up for any shortage of other body-builders such as meat, fish, cheese, milk.

Your allowance of DRIED EGG is equal to 3 eggs a week

You can now get one 12-egg packet (price 1/3) per 4-week rationing period — three fine fresh eggs a week, at the astonishingly low price of 1¼d. each. Children (holders of green ration books) get two packets each rationing period. You buy your dried eggs at the shop where you are registered for shell eggs; poultry keepers can buy anywhere.

Don't hoard your dried eggs; use them up — there are plenty more coming!

Note. *Don't make up dried eggs until you are ready to use them; they should not be allowed to stand after they've been mixed with water or other liquid. Use dry when making cakes and so on, and add a little more moisture when mixing.*

FREE — DRIED EGG LEAFLET containing many interesting recipes, will be sent on receipt of a postcard addressed to Dept. 627E, Food Advice Service, Ministry of Food, London, W.1.

ISSUED BY THE MINISTRY OF FOOD (S.74)

Egg and rice loaf with mushroom sauce is a delicious dish for dinner

DRIED eggs are one of the best foods that wartime rationing has brought us. Always available, always fresh and ready to use, they help the cook in a hundred ways. More than that—they provide every member of the family, from one year old up, with valuable body-building extras for the winter months. Take your full share of dried eggs, learn to use them really well, and you will be doing your household splendid service.

Here are some practical points to remember and some tested recipes for every meal of the day :

When reconstituting dried eggs, first mix the powder to a smooth cream with half the given amount of water, then stir in the remaining liquid. Do not mix the eggs until just before they are needed.

Eggs can be sifted dry into the flour when making batters or "rubbed-in" cake mixtures. For "creamed" cake mixtures, the eggs can be beaten in dry, or reconstituted.

Keep the packet of eggs in a cool dry place, but not in the refrigerator, as they tend to go lumpy.

FOR BREAKFAST :

Bacon Omelette

For two people, allow two reconstituted eggs and

The Mini

What, No Eggs?

A sustaining winter breakfast—savoury egg moulds with sauté potatoes

DRIED EGGS

By Nora Ramsay

(Combined Domestic Science Diploma, Edinburgh)

of bacon, or half a rasher. Cut the ...all pieces and fry in the omelette pan ...Add a nut of fat to cook the omelette, ...hen pour the seasoned eggs into the ...apidly several times with a fork, until ... just set but not brown. Fold up ...n to a hot dish and serve at once.

Egg and Potato Fritters

...ato   1 dried egg
... flour   Dripping or bacon fat (for frying)
...r   Milk if necessary

...r, egg and seasoning into a basin and ...y. Peel the potato, then shred with ...dder into the flour. Make a hollow ... of the ingredients and, if necessary, ...o give a thick batter. Drop spoon-

fuls of the mixture into hot bacon fat or dripping, and fry gently until browned, then turn and fry the other side. Serve immediately. Diced cooked bacon or cold cooked sausage can be added to the fritters, if available.

Parsley Eggs

Reconstitute the desired number of eggs and add seasoning and sufficient chopped parsley to colour green. Steam in a greased egg poacher, or bake in deep patty pans in a moderate oven until set. Turn on to rounds of toast or mashed potatoes, and pour a small spoonful of tomato sauce, mixed with a little piquant sauce, over the top of each egg. Serve very hot.

Potato Surprises

Mix one cupful of mashed potato very thoroughly

with one egg (mixed dry), and season to taste. Add a cooked sausage cut in dice or any small pieces of cooked meat or fish which you have available. Form into flat cakes on a floured board and fry in a little hot fat until lightly browned on both sides. Serve very hot.

FOR LUNCH :

Egg and Rice Loaf

1 pint vegetable boilings	1 tablespoonful chopped
3 oz. rice	onion
3 dried eggs (reconstituted)	1 tablespoonful tomato
1 tablespoonful chopped	sauce
parsley	Seasonings
Parsley or tomato sauce to serve	

Put the rice into a saucepan with the stock, cover and cook gently until the rice is tender and all the stock absorbed. Reconstitute the eggs and add them to the rice with the parsley, onion, tomato sauce and seasonings. Turn into a greased pudding basin or a cake tin and steam or bake in a moderate oven (375° F.) until the mixture is set. This will take about 1 hour. Turn out and serve with parsley or tomato sauce. (Continued on page 102)

of Food has approved this article

◁ △ Although many people were keeping chickens. fresh eggs were rationed for the majority. but in May 1941 the first imports of dried egg powder arrived from America. The initial allowance was one packet. equivalent to 12 eggs. every 8 weeks. later increased to 4 weeks.

What Do I Do With That?

◁ Trying to make some foods sound appetizing wasn't always an easy matter, but the Ministry of Food did their best to encourage experimentation, in this bulletin from 1944.
▷ Fresh fish was scarce, but preserved fish, such as the salted cod from Iceland, was a welcome, if puzzling, addition to the diet. This 1941 article tries to drum up enthusiasm.

How do you Cook Fresh-salted COD?

THE fresh-salted cod which comes from Iceland is a welcome addition to our food supplies at a time when fresh fish is scarce. Priced at a modest d. a pound, it is very good value, as there is practically no waste with it. It is obtainable ready for use from the fishmonger, who washes the salt out of it. Cook on the day it is bought.

Here are some ways of using it, including two quickly made savouries:

Creamed Cod with Tomatoes

1 lb. fresh-salted cod
½ pint milk and water
A bunch of sweet herbs
A sprig of parsley   2 peppercorns
1 bay leaf   1 cupful bottled tomatoes
1 oz. flour   ½ oz. margarine
Sauté potatoes to garnish

Put the cod in a saucepan with the liquid, the herbs and peppercorns tied in muslin, the sprig of parsley and the bay leaf. Cover, and cook very gently until the fish is tender—about 15 minutes. Remove the fish and divide into large flakes. Strain the liquid, and use a little of it to blend the flour for thickening, then put the remaining liquid back in the saucepan with the margarine, and when boiling, stir in the blended flour. Stir and boil for 2 or 3 minutes. Add the flaked fish and the tomatoes (cut in pieces, if necessary) and season to taste. Re-heat, and turn into a hot dish. Garnish with a border of sauté potatoes.

Curried Cod Hot-pot

½ lb. cooked fresh-salted cod
½ lb. cooked carrots
½ pint curry sauce
1 lb. cooked potatoes
A nut of dripping   Brown crumbs

Make a good curry sauce, using some of the fish boilings. Flake the fish, slice the carrots and add both to the sauce, then turn the mixture into a fireproof dish. Cover with a thick layer of sliced cooked potatoes, then sprinkle on a spoonful of browned crumbs and cover with fine shavings of dripping. Put in a hot oven for about 20 minutes, until the potatoes are lightly browned on the top.

Baked Cod au Gratin

1 lb. fresh-salted cod
Little milk and water
½ pint white sauce
2 or 3 oz. grated cheese
1 teaspoonful made mustard   Pepper
1 or 2 teaspoonfuls vinegar
Browned breadcrumbs
A little grated onion, if available

Lay the cod in a greased fireproof dish. Pour round it a little milk and water, cover with margarine paper, and bake in a moderate oven for about 20 minutes, until tender.

Make a white sauce, adding the liquid from the baked fish. Stir in half the grated cheese, the seasonings, the vinegar and the flaked fish. Fill greased scallop shells with the mixture, or place it in a shallow fireproof dish. Sprinkle with the remaining cheese, a few browned crumbs and the grated onion. Bake in a hot oven for about 15 minutes, until golden brown.

Boiled Cod Provençale

1 lb. fresh-salted cod
1 teaspoonful vinegar
A little minced onion, if available
1 oz. margarine
1 or 2 teaspoonfuls salad oil
4 peppercorns (crushed)   Grated nutmeg
1 teaspoonful vinegar or lemon-juice substitute

Put the cod in a saucepan, with cold water to cover and a teaspoonful of vinegar. Bring slowly to boiling-point, and simmer until tender—about 10 minutes. Drain the fish, divide into large flakes and keep hot.

Fry the onion lightly in the margarine, then stir in the salad oil, peppercorns and nutmeg, and mix well. Add the fish, and shake over the heat until thoroughly mixed, without breaking up the flakes. Sprinkle in the parsley, then dish the cod on a bed of nicely mashed potatoes. Serve very hot, sprinkled with vinegar or lemon-juice substitute.

Piquant Fish Toasts

6 rounds of toasted or fried bread
3 oz. cooked fresh-salted cod
1 tablespoonful white sauce
1 tablespoonful tomato sauce or purée
Seasoning
Pickled walnuts, olives, capers or any other pickled vegetable available

Mash the fish, mix with the thick white sauce and the tomato sauce, and season rather highly. Pile the mixture on rounds of toasted or fried bread, and garnish each round with half a pickled walnut or a piece of olive, or decorate with chopped mixed pickles. Place the rounds on a baking tin, cover with margarine paper, heat in a hot oven.

Anchovy Fingers

Scraps of shortcrust pastry
2 oz. of cooked fresh-salted cod
2 tablespoonfuls white sauce flavoured with anchovy essence
A pinch of curry powder
2 salted anchovies or anchovy paste
Chopped parsley

Roll out the pastry ¼ in. thick, cut in fingers and bake in a hot oven. Mash the fish and mix with the anchovy sauce. Add curry powder to taste. Wash and pound the salted anchovies, and mix into the sauce. (If anchovy paste is used, spread this on the pastry fingers.) Pile the fish mixture neatly on the pastry. Reheat in a hot oven, garnish with parsley.

Paper is a munition of war—never waste a scrap.

Precious CRUSTS

No scrap of bread is too small to save — it means saving valuable shipping space. Of course your best and most direct way of helping, is to take less bread into the house. Most households find they can do nicely with three-quarters of the bread they used to buy and yet can give every member of the family all the bread he or she individually needs.

The secret is in eating up every scrap of bread that comes in. Don't forget the end of the loaf. It's the bit that's apt to get left over. You always intended to do something with it. But how often was it thrown out, after all !

Half a slice of stale bread saved by everyone in this country every day, means a convoy of 30 ships a year freed to take munitions or men to our fighting fronts. If you explain this to your family you'll find them eager enough to help you save on bread !

Save Bread : Save Ships

4 things you can do

1 **Cut down your purchase (or making) of bread.** Most households find they can do nicely with three-quarters of the bread they used to buy.

2 Put the loaf on the dresser or side table. Cut only as required.

3 Use every crumb.

4 Don't eat bread whilst potatoes are on the table.

Some ways of using up STALE BREAD

CRISPY PIE-CRUST . Cut bread into dice $\frac{1}{4}$ in. thick. Cover a savoury pie with them, setting the dice closely together. Pour over them a little thin custard (salted) taking care that every piece of bread is moistened. Bake in a brisk oven.

SOAKED BREAD. This is the foundation of a countless number of puddings and cakes. No bread is too stale for it, and there is no need to remove any crust. Break into small pieces, put into bowl, cover completely with cold water and soak thoroughly. If the bread is to be used for a savoury, use vegetable boilings instead of water. Then squeeze the bread *hard*, put back in the bowl and beat with a fork until quite free from lumps and pieces of crust. The beating is most important and makes all the difference between a dull heavy pudding and a smooth, spongy texture.

MINCE SLICES — AND — MAKING RUSKS

Mix 8 ozs. mince with 4 ozs. cooked mashed potatoes and 4 ozs. fine crumbs. Season to taste. Roll out on a floured board into an oblong $\frac{1}{4}$ in. thick. Cut into slices and fry in a very little hot fat or grill for 5 to 7 mins. Serve with leek sauce.

Cut bread into neat figures, or fancy shapes, about $\frac{1}{2}$ in thick. Bake in a warm oven until crisp and golden brown. Pack in an air-tight tin. This is a valuable emergency store which will keep good for months.

TURN WASTE INTO DELICACIES !

(S.61)   ISSUED BY THE MINISTRY OF FOOD

Take pride in your Patchwork.

Meals out of doors will help you to enjoy this summer *more!*

THE good your food does you depends a lot on the way you live. Sunshine, fresh air, a happy atmosphere, sleep, an occasional change of surroundings — all play their part in what scientists call "nutrition."

Meals out of doors make a welcome change from routine; and give you an extra ration of vitamin D because the action of sunlight on the skin enables the body to make its own vitamin in addition to that which you get from food.

So get out of doors as much as you can this summer — even if it's mostly in the garden — and you will build up health for the winter as well as enjoy this summer more.

Camp Fire Cooking

This is one of the delights of childhood that even adults never grow out of. Frying sausages, baking potatoes in the hot embers of a fire — boiling the kettle for tea!

If you have a Scout or Guide in the family, they'll build the regulation fire. Or if you're ambitious, you may like to build a more permanent outdoor cooker (useful as a garden incinerator, too).

You can get particulars of how to do this from your local W.V.S. Take care not to let any fire get out of control and, of course, make sure it's thoroughly out by black-out time.

Picnic Meals

Sandwiches are easier to make if, when spreading the margarine, you dip the knife in boiling water. Dried egg makes a good filling: use cold scrambled egg, or reconstituted egg steamed in small greased cups. When set, turn out and slice for your sandwiches.

Or make Scotch eggs by covering the steamed egg with sausage meat; then fry.

Salads make substantial meals if you add some cann— or cooked fish or meat, or cold bacon, or gra— cheese or egg. Serve with bread and butter or margarine and a milky drink.

Hot Meals, too

When you cook a hot meal indoors, choose one that can "take care of itself," so that you are not tied to the kitchen. For instance, a casserole main dish, root vegetables in a little water in covered baking dishes, and a milk pudding, can be left in a low oven without constant watching.

Suggested Me—
Holidays at H—

A leaflet cont—
many useful ti—
recipes glad—
on receipt —
card. Pleas—
"Suggested—
for Holi—
Home" an—
Food Ad—
sion, De—
Ministry —
London —

Let's talk about

XMAS FOOD

There won't be turkey on many tables this year; but the Christmas atmosphere will be there and the children's eyes will sparkle gaily. From what we know of you, you'll make your Christmas catering a grand success in spite of difficulties, and we're out to help you all we can. Here are a few suggestions of general interest from letters we have sent to correspondents. A Happy Christmas to you!

I'd like a recipe for Christmas pudding without eggs.
Mix together 1 cupful of flour, 1 cupful of sugar, half a cupful of breadcrumbs, 1 cupful of suet, 1 cupful of mixed dried fruit; and, if you like, 1 teaspoonful of mixed sweet spice. Then add 1 cupful of grated potato, 1 cupful of grated raw carrot, and finally 1 level teaspoonful of bicarbonate of soda dissolved in 2 tablespoonfuls of hot milk. Mix all together (no further moisture if necessary), turn into a well-greased pudding basin. Boil or steam for 4 hours.

SOME HINTS FOR CHILDREN'S PARTY FOOD, PLEASE!

Chocolate squares are popular. Melt 3 oz. margarine with two tablespoonfuls of syrup in a saucepan, mix in 1 cupful of rolled oats and a pinch of salt. Blend well and put in a greased, shallow baking tin, flattening the mixture smoothly. Bake half an hour to 40 minutes in a moderate oven. Take out, and while still hot grate over it a tablet of chocolate. The chocolate will evenly with a knife. Cut into squares and lift out.

Amusing little figures, cut from short-crust or biscuit dough, go down well. Roll the dough about 1/4-inch thick. People make them by cutting small rounds for bodies, strips for arms and legs; place the various pieces of dough firmly together. Prick out eyes, nose, mouths, with currants. If you can make a little or have a friend who can, make this cardboard patterns of animals, lay them on the dough and cut round with a small sharp knife.

Chocolate coating for your Christmas cake. Mix together 3 tablespoonfuls of sugar with a table-spoonful of cocoa and 2 tablespoonfuls of milk. Stir, in a stout saucepan,

oxay low heat until the mixture is thick and bubbly like toffee; then, while hot, pour it over your cake.

A Christmassy sparkle is easy to give to sprigs of holly or evergreen for use on puddings and cakes. Dip your greenery in a strong solution of Epsom salts. When dry it will be beautifully frosted.

I'll miss my gay bowl of fruit on the Christmas table. Now in its place, why not have a bowl of salad in its colours—vegetables are such jolly colours—the cheerful glow of carrot, the rich crimson of beetroot, the emerald parsley. And better still, make you should have a winter salad every so far, one meal a day. Here's a suggestion; it looks as delightful as it tastes.

Salad slices. Cut a thick round of wheatmeal bread and spread it with spread with margarine each person and of tomato and the centre of each slice, and, if liked, put a sardine on it. Surround with circles of grated carrot, chopped parsley, raw celery, finely chopped parsley or spinach and grated raw beetroot on the edge. Sprinkle with a little grated cheese.

Issued by The Ministry of Food.

Food, Glorious Food

◁▷ During the war priority for advertising space in the magazine was given to the various ministries. Through their bulletins, the Ministry of Food informed the public on matters such as nutrition, food issues and economies, and provided recipes and answers to questions from consumers.

Health for Victory

It is no exaggeration to say that Victory itself depends on healthful meals, for it will come to the nations which show the greatest power of endurance, stamina and will-power. To conserve this strength, the smaller trials of life, such as instability of temper, mental depression, and physical fatigue, must be overcome, and this can be accomplished to a surprising extent by the housewife. Her medicine does not come from the bottle, but from the plate, three times daily. She knows that the food which simply satisfies hunger is not necessarily correct : on the contrary, the food that makes one feel energetic and intelligent helps most to resist disease, while indigestion from unsuitable food robs even the bravest Cockney of his sense of humour !

The Ministry of Food has

Pickling isn't the only way of dealing with red cabbage. It is very good served hot, and makes a delicious foundation for these Cheese Dumplings

Meals for Victory

E. Himsworth

...ician

...ME Ministry of Food campaigns...
...here are three classes of food:

1. *Fuel Foods*, that is, star...
...rt from fats, we take adequate...
...bothering much about them.

...*Body-building Foods*, or the a...
...dairy produce) and the pulses;...
...hese if we are taking our full...

...*Protective Foods*, containing...
...s, which, as the name suggests, p...
...ciencies or special illness, e.g...
...s, anæmia, etc.

...is the last group which, th...
...ith, is so often lacking. It i...
...efore, when planning her menu...
...icular group, for the rest will,...
...r itself.

...he protective foods are natura...
...a) The garden or market gard...
...vegetables.
...b) The sea, oily fishes being th...
...c) The dairy, which supplies m...
...margarine. These foods are...

One Ounce Per Head

IF you were to serve a four-ounce piece of fish or meat in solitary state to a company of four people, it might reasonably be thought that something had "gone wrong" with the housekeeping. Yet, dietetically, one ounce of protein food (meat, fish, cheese, etc.) per head for a supper or luncheon dish is a fair allowance, if supplemented with vegetables, and so on. It only requires a little ingenuity to serve it in such a way as to make it appear—and prove—satisfying.

The recipes that follow are based on this allowance. The quantities given are for four persons, so each recipe contains four ounces of the main protein ingredient.

FOUR OUNCES OF STEAK . . .

Here is an excellent way of dealing with a slice of stewing steak, with four alternative ways of serving it.

Rolled Steak

4-oz. piece of steak (cut in one thin slice)
½ oz. dripping
1 stick celery, 1 leek and 1 or 2 carrots, all minced
Salt and pepper
Few cooked haricots
Fresh herbs (parsley, thyme, etc.)
4 oz. short-crust pastry, if the roll is to be baked
or
4 oz. suet-crust pastry, if the roll is to be steamed

Lay the piece of steak on a board and beat with a rolling pin to a thickness of about ⅛ in. To make the stuffing, sauté the minced celery, leek and carrots in the dripping for about 5 minutes, then add a good sprinkling of chopped fresh herbs. Add the mashed haricots and seasoning and mix well.

Place this stuffing in the centre of the piece of steak, then roll the meat over it and tie up securely with string or thread, like a parcel.

The roll may be cooked in four different ways:

(1) Roast for ¾ hour in a strong, covered saucepan with a little dripping, turning it at frequent intervals. Serve with plenty of vegetables (which may be cooked in the pan with the meat, if liked) and a rich gravy made from the dripping.

(2) Stew for about 1½ hours, in a good brown sauce with mixed vegetables, frying the roll to a golden-brown in the dripping before making the sauce.

(3) Steam the roll, first encasing it in pastry crust. Make 4 oz. suet-crust pastry in the usual way, roll it out about ⅛ in. thick and wrap the meat roll in it, moistening the edges of the

pastry where it joins (there is no nee... to string the meat roll first). Wrap i... greased paper, tie in a cloth and stea... for about 2 hours. Serve with vege... tables and a sauce or gravy.

(4) Bake the roll in the oven. F... this you need 4 oz. shortcrust pastr... (made, if possible, from wheatme... flour), rolled into an oblong, abou... ⅛ in. in thickness, and wrapped roun... the meat roll (again there is no nee... to tie the meat first with string o... thread). Place on a greased bakin... sheet and bake in a hot oven (450° F... until lightly browned, reducing th... temperature of 375° F. until cooke... through—about 1 hour in all. Serv... with vegetables and a sauce or gravy...

FOUR OUNCES OF CORNED BEE... OR GALANTINE . . .

There are other ways of servin... corned beef and tinned galantines tha... cold with vegetables or salad. R... member that the meat is alread... cooked, so that dishes containing... are quick and easy to prepare. Ou... second recipe is a variation of a dis... very popular in America: Corned Bee... Hash.

Creamed Galantine

4 oz. galantine or corned beef
½ pint milk
½ pint vegetable stock
1 oz. flour—good measure
½ oz. margarine
Salt and pepper
½ teaspoonful mad... mustard
1 bunch watercres...
2 Spring onions, finel... chopped

The dustbin that holds more than ash to-day is a reproach.

...but-liver Oil. Wise housewives ... "Points" to the greatest advantage by purchasing tinned pilchards, sardines, salmon, fish roe, etc., when fresh varieties are not available.

Cod-liver oil, even the more or less tasteless variety now procurable, may not be appreciated by the family, but you can overcome this by using it for cooking purposes, in fish sauce or in mayonnaise. (Continued on page 75)

The flavour of cod-liver oil is practically indistinguishable when used in salad dressing

◁ △ 1942: Despite the limited supplies of food and its lack of variety, the message was continually drummed into people that a healthy nation was a victorious one.

BRITAIN'S
CIVIL ARMY

too, marches on its stomach!

On the Food Front

△ ▷ By 1944 the majority of people were employed in some capacity, whether in the home, factory or doing war work, and canteen cooking on a budget was the subject of numerous articles, as was finding the time to cook nourishing meals.

Students at work in the new Good Housekeeping Canteen Cookery School

Catering for War-Workers

Practical Advice from Good Housekeeping Institute

By producing each day one substantial meal containing all the essential nutrients, the Canteen Cook helps to maintain the morale and efficiency of the Home Front. Menus must be carefully planned, and the rations eked out with plenty of protective foods (e.g. potatoes, vegetables, oatmeal and National bread) and quantities carefully estimated—bearing in mind that when numbers are increased, catering is more economical, and a rather smaller proportion of food may be allowed per head. Here are some hints for those newly embarked on such work :

To Eke Out the Meat Ration

1. Serve plenty of vegetables, preferably serving both root and green vegetables at each main meal.

2. Use oatmeal or wholemeal flour for thickening soups and stews.

3. Serve meatless dishes, using cheese, pulses and milk in order to maintain the body-building value of the meal.

4. Follow a vegetable dish with a satisfying pudding.

5. Use as much internal meat as possible—these meats are all highly nutritious.

6. Mix minced vegetables or fine sago with minced meat, allowing 2 oz. to 1 lb. of mince, when using it for filling pasties, roly-poly, etc.

Mix oatmeal with mince, allowing 2 oz. oatmeal to 1 lb. mince, for " Mince Collops."

Add mashed potatoes or cooked vegetables to mince, when making meat cakes, baked meat loaf, etc.

7. Pay great care to the thorough flavouring and seasoning of all vegetable dishes.

To Save Fat

1. Bake rissoles, fish, cutlets, etc., instead of frying.

2. If a good filling is used, scones and rolls for mid-morning snacks or tea will require little or no fat.

General Hints

1. The use of custard powder in milk puddings in the proportion of $\frac{1}{4}$ lb. custard powder to $2\frac{1}{2}$ lb. grain will help to make them more egg-like in appearance.

2. When making sauces and milk puddings, prepare them early in the day and cook slowly in either some form of bain-marie or a steamer. If cooking on a fuel cooker, whole-rice puddings can be cooked in large basins on top.

* Make your dustbin serve Britain's arsenal.

KIA-ORA
*looks
forward!*

KEEPS WAR WORKERS "FIGHTING FIT"

*The Human
machine needs
ENERGY too*

War workers—try Weetabix! Have it at breakfast, take it
to the factory or workshop, eat some, *some time*, every day.
You'll find it delicious and—vitally more important—
wonderfully sustaining. Weetabix is wheat, the whole
of the wheat, with all its valuable mineral salts and
Vitamins intact. This makes Weetabix so nourishing,
so energising, and will make *you* so much better able to do
your war job.

Weetabix
More than a breakfast food

| SMALL SIZE 7½d. 2 points |
| LARGE SIZE 1/1 4 points |

Weetabix Ltd., Burton Latimer, Northants.
W x2

△ ▷ Advertising was frequently
patriotic. with war a recurring
theme. Advertisers emphasized the
part their products had played in
the war effort by using images of
servicemen and women and. as in
the 1945 advertisement. right.
messages explaining the product's
continued absence from the shelves.

Their Finest Hour

Now it can be told . . .

Many of the Heinz Varieties that you could not get for so long have been on Service with the Forces. Here is a list of what they have had, and, knowing Heinz quality, you can judge what has been done to keep them 'fighting fit':

SELF-HEATING CANS

of Kidney Soup, Cream of Green Pea Soup, Mock Turtle Soup, Cream of Celery Soup, Oxtail Soup, Cream of Chicken Soup, Cocoa Milk, Malt Milk.

DEHYDRATED VEGETABLES

Potato, Carrot, Cabbage.

OTHER VARIETIES

Baked Beans — Tomato Soup — Celery Soup — Minced Beef and Vegetables — Savoury Rice and Sausages — Corned Beef Hash — Stewed Steak — Canned Mutton — Pork and Vegetables — Beef Stew — Boiled Beef, Carrots and Dumplings — Meat and Vegetable Ration — Steak and Kidney Pudding — Mutton Broth — Treacle Pudding — Mixed Fruit Pudding — Marmalade Pudding — Rice Pudding — Sultana Pudding — Date Pudding — Vegetable Salad — Sausages —Chicken and Ham Paste—Spaghetti—Coffee.

HEINZ
57

Always ready to serve..

BOVRIL puts the best face on Vegetables

TAKE A TEASPOONFUL OF BOVRIL AND S...

Go easy with BREAD eat POTATOES instead

BOVRIL

MANUFACTURED
BOVRIL LTD LONDON
ENGLAND

Vegetable dishes made with Bovril will surprise you with their flavour and goodness. It's the concentrated essence of prime lean beef that does it—helps you not only to enjoy but to assimilate your food. And fortunately Bovril is still to be had in reasonable quantities.

BOVRIL improves the dish

(Obtainable in 1oz., 2oz., 4oz. & 8oz. Bottles)

TOTAL WAR EFFORT
demands the withdrawal
of 'Golden Shred'

The World's Best Marmalade

It will return with
VICTORY

JAMES ROBERTSON & SONS (P.M.) Ltd.
Golden Shred Works

Paisley   Manchester   Bristol

Please leave Horlicks for those who need it most

ONE REASON why Horlicks is scarce is that it is included in emergency rations supplied to sailors and airmen, who may have to live for many days without normal supplies of food. Horlicks also goes to hospitals, to certain war factories, and to miners. Nevertheless, some Horlicks is still being supplied to the shops. Please leave it for those who need it most. And make Horlicks by mixing it with water only. The milk is already...

..you lucky people

...I've found a tin of
Nescafé

A cup of good coffee, fragrant and stimulating, made in a jiffy, right in the cup! Nescafé, concentrated coffee in powder form, is indeed a boon; no mess, no grounds; no bother. But unfortunately it is not possible, under present conditions, to supply increasing demand; grocers must be rationed. Still, what a lucky thing when you *do* get a tin of Nescafé!

N.1

NESCAFÉ
A NESTLÉ'S PRODUCT

THIS IS IDRIS SPEAKING. GIVING YOU THE NEWS . . .

SORRY . . UNTIL PEACE RETURNS THERE WILL BE NO MORE
IDRIS
THE QUALITY SOFT DRINK

◁ △ Many foodstuffs were unavailable or in short supply during the war. This Bovril advert from 1944 is typical in trying to reassure customers that the product is still available. despite the shortages. Other adverts apologise for the lack of supplies and promise a return to normal service after the war.

We'll Eat
Again

FOR
JELLY
SURPRISES

**To make these
JELLY EGGS**

Take one of the two sections of Bird's
Jelly-de-Luxe and dissolve. Fill Egg
Cups to the brim and allow to set. Turn
out on to a plate. Dissolve other
section of jelly and fill Egg Cups
to within ¼ inch of top and allow to
set. Lift turned-out shapes with a
knife and place on set jelly in Egg Cups.

.. there's nothing like

BIRD'S
JELLY-DE-LUXE

We're Still Around

△ ▽ Some luxury items were still around for a while to brighten the drab diet, but November 1941 saw canned food rationed and in August 1942 biscuits followed suit.

WARTIME
Fashion & Beauty

Their houses and families may have been ravaged by the scourge of war, but the women of Britain were determined that their appearance did not suffer the same fate. Whether at home or involved in war work for the services, every effort was made to maintain their looks whatever the conditions: 'Put your best face forward' a Yardley cosmetics advertisement demands.

As with food and cooking, the shortages demanded scrimping, saving and ingenuity. Advertisements found in *Good Housekeeping* at the time emphasize the need to 'Cherish your Perfume – Treasure your Powder'. Some go as far as to admit that supplies are short but will be in ample supply after the war. But elsewhere they are more expansive, littered with poetic quotations – 'Is she not more than painting can express', hinting at the escapism that a dash of lipstick provided in the midst of such hardship.

Put your best face forward...

Because the loveliness they give seems truly natural, Yardley beauty-things are more precious today than ever.

Remember, they still have all the qualities you know and trust.

Yardley

33 OLD BOND STREET · LONDON

May th

● White satin and orange blossom
are still first favourites with Service
brides: the dress on the opposite
page in gleaming slipper satin has
a softly gathered corsage tying with a
bow at the back. Bourne & Hollings-
worth. Seven coupons, £8 2s. 6d.
● The girl who chooses her dress
with an eye to its immediate after-use
will like the dusty pink rayon crêpe
frock above. Golflaine's Slimuette,
from John Barker. Seven coupons,
£3 14s. 2d. The elegant D. Carlton
hat is in fine black straw. ● Another practical choice for to-day's
bride is a Selita Utility jumper-suit,
right, in turquoise-coloured fine wool
with frilled waistcoat points. John
Lewis. Fourteen coupons; about
£3. The tiny hat massed with
summer flowers is from D. Carlton.

The Service Bride

un shine ...

△ With no extra coupons issued for wedding dresses, service brides-to-be often chose their outfits with an eye to the future and reuse, such as the ones shown above left from June 1944. For many, honeymoons might be just a snatched 48-hour leave.

FOR THE
MOTHER-TO-BE

In dull tartan checks, a well-cut Utility tweed coat (below, right) can be worn slimly belted or as a concealing swagger. Treasure Cot. 18 coupons. £4 10s. 6d. The little boy wears a Buster Utility suit from Treasure Cot, blue and white striped shirt and lined trousers in butcher blue. 4 coupons. 10s. 2d. Size 16.

Chalk-stripes are used in an interesting way on this pleated woollen frock and its matching jacket in red, navy, brown or green. Individually made to measure by Du Barry. 19 coupons. £12 14s. 10d.

◁ ▽ Having just 66 clothing coupons a year was no incentive to splash out on maternity wear, but the mother-to-be wanted clothes that could be altered once baby was born: companies such as DuBarry offered a remodelling service.
▷ Those women not lucky enough to have the luxury of a pair of stockings – such as those offered by Wolsey in 1942 – could always use leg make-up and draw in the seams.

HAPPY EVENT!

A MOTHER-TO-BE, and she looks her prettiest! All DU BARRY MODELS are designed on a patented principle (Patent No. 2811) which makes them comfortable and concealing. Come and try on some of the really smart styles or send for beautiful folio of designs. The dress as sketched, in Matt Crepe in lovely range of colours— 5 gns.

COUPON ECONOMY
Du Barry's Coupon-Free Department will remodel your dress after the event.

DuBarry
MATERNITY WEAR

MAYfair 0118
DU BARRY—New Showroom

Looking Smart

Brevets

Wolsey Shirtmaker

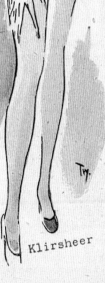

Klirsheer

Coupon wizards by Wolsey

SUMMER CHARMERS

Value-PLUS washing frocks, crisply tailored, with a beautiful expensive-looking finish, from linen-like Moygashel "Non-krush" rayon.

At left, light top, dark skirt in luscious colour combinations, as pastel blue / wine; ice pink / blackberry; lemon / rust; pastel blue / tan; cream / navy. Sizes 38/42-in. hips.

At right, solid colour with hand-drawn-thread decorated bodice: navy, rust, mid-green, lemon, ice pink and pastel blue. Sizes 36/42-in. hips.

Both "Utility" frocks, of course. Look for the double label, "C. C. Chabut" model. From Peter Robinsons, Oxford Circus, W.1, and good shops over the country. Each 56s.

◁ In May 1942 Utility clothing was introduced. Designed to be functional and to minimize the use of cloth that was in short supply, it raised hemlines and banished double-breasted styles and turnups on trousers. It was available with coupons.

▽ ▷ Advertisements from 1942 extolling the virtues of Utility clothing.

● Despite the fourth year of war, Wolsey Shirtmakers maintain their high standard. For out-of-doors during early autumn, and in the house all winter long, these dresses are an excellent " buy " and well worth the investment of eleven coupons. From the wide range of colours, the girl on the left has chosen willow green. ● On the right is another of the many designs, in smoke grey, enlivened with an emerald suède belt.

37

STEVENSON'S MOYGASHEL 'NON-KRUSH' 'UTILITY' RAYONS

QUANTITY CONTROLLED BUT NOT QUALITY...

We thank all users of MOYGASHEL fabrics throughout the country for their support in the past and assure them that although quantities produced will be much restricted this year, we shall do our utmost to satisfy their needs. Should they, however, have been unable to obtain MOYGASHEL fabrics, we ask their indulgence. We look forward with sure confidence to the time when production of MOYGASHEL fabrics will again be unrestricted.

STEVENSON & SON, LTD
11, Argyll Street, London, W.1
LONDON, NEW YORK, DUNGANNON

Utility Clothing

Matelot : Feminine version of a Free French sailor's cap, with lots of style. This takes 3 oz. 4-ply wool to crochet

Minx : *A saucy snood that keeps your hair away from your neck and has a becoming silhouette.* Use silky bouclé yarn

Magpie : *Cool and light on the hottest day, a " mortar-board " beret crocheted in white cotton, with contrasting feather*

CROCHET HOOKS FORWARD!

All you who can crochet get busy with one, at least of these three delightful hat designs. They are easy to do and work out very inexpensive. Full directions for all three designs in Bulletin No. 48, 6d. post free obtainable from the Good Housekeeping Needlework Department, 28–30 Grosvenor Gardens, London, S.W.

MAKE YOUR CHOICE AN

* Make SALVAGE part of your Household routine.

A Head for Fashion

the *Hat Parade*

HOME MILLINERS MOBILISE!

Hats are a strain on the budget these days, so launch out and make your own. The three styles shown on this page were designed by a famous West End milliner, to be carried out by those with no millinery experience or specialised equipment. Full instructions on page 64.

Flirt : Pretty as a picture and wonderfully light and " comfy " to wear. Rayon straw braid by the yard is the material to use here

Flatterer : A profile beret particularly becoming to those with irregular features who cannot wear " off face " styles. Make it from piece petersham or firm taffeta, preferably dark-toned

Fez : Equally smart with suit or dress. A cute pill-box fez styled in New York. Make it in felt with piping cord trim

SAVE YOUR SHILLINGS!

* Waste Paper is War Paper.

27

△ Crocheted, knitted and felt hats were just some of the fashions in 1942 – making your own meant saving money and coupons.

Entrances and Exits . . . The world is full of people—yet on this day there is only one woman and one man. Together and happy—walking away with merit rewarded. Such a day is one to be remembered, a day when above all others you must walk your best—with the ease and comfort, for instance, that Vani-tred shoes give. . . .

DALE 2

Balanced Walking VANI-TRED *Shoes*

VANI-TRED SHOES (C.V.8) 17/18 OLD BOND STREET, LONDON, W.1. (WHOLESALE ONLY)

Best Foot Forward

△ An ad from 1944. Designed to be practical, shoes had low or medium heels. Cork platforms were popular, but wooden shoes took a bit of getting used to. ▷ Buying shoes required coupons, and one way to save was to make your own, as this article from July 1943 shows – fashion had to be sacrificed.

Make Your Own Sandals

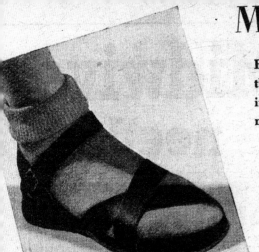

R. C. D. TOVEY tells you how to save coupons by making these smart leather sandals. They are quite easy to make if you follow the instructions carefully and, like all hand-made articles, will give you a good deal of hard wear

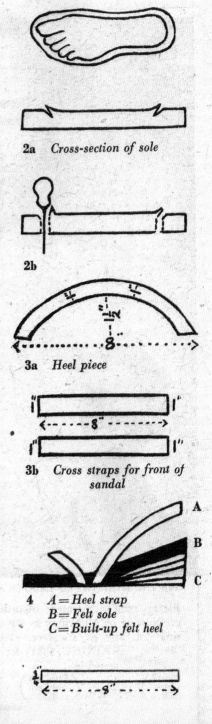

2a   *Cross-section of sole*

2b

3a   *Heel piece*

3b   *Cross straps for front of sandal*

4   A = *Heel strap*
B = *Felt sole*
C = *Built-up felt heel*

erials required :

ne piece of sole leather, suffi-
for two soles. Thick felt
inner soles. Scraps of soft
er for straps. Four "wax-
" complete with needles (ob-
ble from saddler's shop).
awl. Pliers.

ections

rst you must cut out the
. If you have a pair of old
als this is easy, since you
ely need to pencil round
m on the leather. If not, trace
outline of your bare foot
piece of paper and round it
o sandal shape, as shown in
1. Cut out this paper pat-
and draw around it firmly
the leather, then turn the
er over and draw the other
. (*Note*—The pattern *must*
eversed for the second sole,
rwise you will have two left
ight soles instead of a pair.)
t out the soles along these
kings with a very sharp knife
heavy clasp knife is best, if
can borrow one. Then draw
e roughly ¼ in. from the edge
nd the bottom of the sole
shiny side) and cut around
with the knife for about
n. in a slanting direction—
is, not ⅛ in. deep, but so
there is a flap of leather
wide which can be slightly
ed (see Fig. 2a).

Now with the bradawl make
holes ³⁄₁₆ in. apart all round the
sole, lifting the little flap just
made, inserting the point of the
bradawl underneath, and push-
ing through to the other side of
the sole (Fig. 2b).

Cut felt inner soles exactly
the same size as the leather
ones, but do not make holes
or cut flaps in these. Put
your foot on the felt sole and
experiment with the placing of
strips cut from newspaper according to the diagrams 3a and 3b.
Remember that the strips should
be sufficiently long to allow of
¾ in. being tucked underneath
the felt on each side. Having
made any necessary adjustments
in the paper patterns, mark them
out on the soft leather and cut
them out with scissors. Pin the
ends of the leather strips under
the felt sole and see that they
fit properly and are in the right
position; then sew the ends
firmly to the underside of the
felt with thread, and remove the
pins.

Cut several pieces of felt
(according to the required thickness of the heel) from half the
pattern of the sole (i.e. from the
heel to instep) and tack these together. With a sharp knife pare
down the thicknesses of felt at
the instep, so that there is a
gradual slope, and tack this heel
wedge under the inner sole (diagram 4).

Place the inner and outer soles
together and fix in position by
means of string tied around the
instep, or the spring type of paper
clip. (*Continued on page* 55)

△ If you weren't handy with a needle and thread. many companies offered their services in remodelling your old clothes.

▽ For those who could sew. *Good Housekeeping* provided lots of ideas for bringing glamour to outdated outfits. such as this one from November 1943.

THIS SEWING CAMPA

22

Take a dated glamour-jacket of long-haired fur and bring to a high standard of usefulness with a few pieces of firmly-woven fabric. Add deep cuffs to the three-quarter or seven-eighth sleeves, drawn into a but-toned band, stitch a scarf-length to the collarless neck and gather the lower edge into a snug waistband, buttoning at front.

Make Do and Mend

◁ Make-do-and-mend parties among friends and neighbours were encouraged. as this article from January 1943 illustrates.

▽ Made from scraps of wool and cotton. this pullover from 1943 would certainly have got you noticed.

WE cannot all be skilled dressmakers, but every woman can learn to mend, alter and renovate her clothes, especially if experience and materials, too, are pooled. Get together with your friends and plan make-do-and-mend parties. It's a good way to save fuel and give worn clothes a new lease of life at one and the same time.

The girls in the picture opposite, planning a sewing campaign, wear contrasting types of woollen dresses. Left, a soft, feminine dress of fine black wool with gathered front panels of maize-yellow. A Roter model. Right, for those who like tailored clothes, a trim shirt-woollen in a grey honeycomb jersey; Wolsey. Above: the women who prefer suits to dresses will appreciate the classic cut of this all-occasions Harella suit in black, red and white gun-club checked tweed.

Supplies of the models shown cannot be guaranteed, but the Clothes Consultant will be glad to give names of stockists where possible. Please send a stamped addressed envelope.

Exercise to keep fit—and warm.   23

Take one or more tired frocks and spice them up with a cheerful sleeveless pullover made from the brightest scraps of woollen in your piece-box. Cut strips, join them by machine in the gayest colour combination you can manage, then cut out your pullover from this length of material. Line with oddment of strong cotton or woollen for firmness and extra warmth.

Presents

FOR GOOD LITTLE GIRLS AND BOYS— CUDDLESOME, LOVABLE

HAND-KNITTED TOYS

Full instructions for making these popular and practical knitted toys in Bulletin No. 45.

They take odd lengths and left-overs of wool only, and are quite simple to do.

Send 9d. in stamps to Good Housekeeping Needlework Dept., 28–30 Grosvenor Gardens, London, S.W.1, asking for Bulletin No. 45.

KNIT SOMETHING FOR A PRESENT—

STRIPED JUMPER AND GLOVES

Materials : 6 oz. Patons Super, or Beehive, Scotch Fingering 3-ply, in various shades. A pair each Nos. 11 and 10 Beehive 9-inch needles, and a set of 4 No. 11 needles, pointed both ends. A No. 11 crochet hook. 4 buttons.

Measurements : *Jumper.* To fit 32-34-in. bust ; length from top of shoulder, 19 in., sleeve seam, 4 in. *Gloves.* To fit 6½-7 hand (length of fingers adjustable).

Tension : 6 sts. to an inch before pressing. *N.B.*—Arrange coloured stripes as required.

Abbreviations : St. = stitch ; k. = knit ; p. = purl ; in. = inches ; tog. = together ; wl. fwd. = wool forward ; rep. = repeat ; inc. = increase(ing).

This gay jumper and glove set may be made from oddments of wool: instructions herewith

—AND SOMETHING FOR YOURSELF

JUMPER

Back and Front (both alike). With No. 11 needles cast on 84 sts. and work 4 in. in k. 1, p. 1 rib. Change to No. 10 needles :
1st and 2nd rows : K. *3rd row :* K. 1, * k. 2 tog., wl. fwd. ; rep. from * to last st., k. 1. *4th row :* K. Rep. these 4 rows, inc. at each end of 12th and every following 6th row until there are 98 sts. on needle. Work straight until side edge measures 12 in.

Shape armholes : Cast off 4 sts. at beginning of next 2 rows, then k. 2 tog. at each end of alternate rows till 74 sts. remain. Work straight until work measures 18¾ in.

Shape shoulders : Cast off 12 sts. at beginning of next 4 rows. Cast off.

SLEEVES

With No. 11 needles cast on 60 sts. and work 1 in. in k. 1, p. 1 rib. Change to No. 10 needles and pattern, inc. at each end of every 4th row until there are 72 sts. Work straight until side edge measures 4 ins.

(Continued on page 45)

And then you'll stand a chance of dodging death upon the road.

The two smaller pho[to]
show garments whi[ch]
on Bulletins. The [...]
with cable stitch yol[ke ...]
30 ; made to fit a [...]
bust, it takes 8 [...]
Laine " Super [...]
3-ply. The bedja[cket ...]
[Bul]letin No. 31, takes [...]
Templeton's " [...]
Fingering 3-ply, [...]
34–36-in. bust. [...]
Bulletin, post [...]
Good Housekeep[ing ...]
Grosvenor Garde[ns ...]

◁ Many children's toys were unavailable, but one solution was to use odd ends or leftovers of wool to create colourful knitted toys.

△ These tops from 1941 could be knitted with oddments, while to buy wool would cost 1 coupon for 2oz.

Get Knitting

A new hair style is as exciting as a new hat—
and generally speaking far cheaper. In these days you
can wear your hair up, down, round, wavy,
curly, straight. The variety is enormous, the choice
is a test of your intelligent interest in making yourself
as pretty as possible. Study these sketches, decide on
the shape and lines of your head, and style your hair to—

Round face

FLATTER YOUR FACE

Long face

FIRST, the shape from the front. Yours is a round face? Then pile your curls high, with flat up-brushed wings above the temples. A long face? Minimise the length with a curled-under fringe, a page-boy roll circling and framing your cheeks. That difficult "egg" shape, wider across the jaw than the forehead? Build up width at the sides and top. Heart shape? You are fortunate—you can have a tumble of curls for its own sake, and if summer tempts you to tie them off your forehead with a narrow ribbon bow, you'll look more engagingly heart-shaped than ever.

By
Muriel Cox

46

Egg-shaped

Heart-shaped

Hairstyles to Flatter

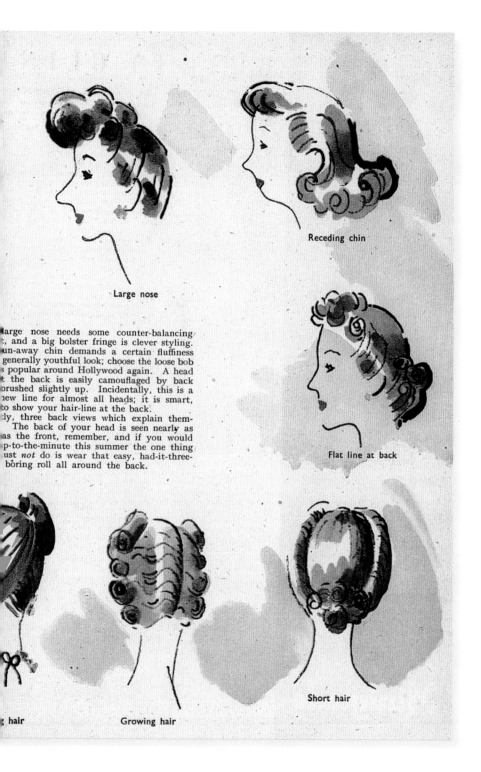

Receding chin

Large nose

Flat line at back

Large nose needs some counter-balancing
, and a big bolster fringe is clever styling.
un-away chin demands a certain fluffiness
generally youthful look; choose the loose bob
popular around Hollywood again.   A head
the back is easily camouflaged by back
rushed slightly up.   Incidentally, this is a
ew line for almost all heads; it is smart,
o show your hair-line at the back.
ly, three back views which explain them-
The back of your head is seen nearly as
as the front, remember, and if you would
p-to-the-minute this summer the one thing
ust *not* do is wear that easy, had-it-three-
boring roll all around the back.

hair

Growing hair

Short hair

△ Wearing your hair short or up was as much a
safety measure as a fashion statement. With more
women doing factory work, accidents caused by long
hair being caught in machines had become frequent.

Perennial Beauty

Violet sweetest flower of the English spring, symbol of truth, modesty, and innocence, inspiration of lyric poetry in every age — fit name for the sweet and lovely woman whose beauty is in the care of

Snowfire

BEAUTY PREPARATIONS

We regret that Snowfire Beauty Preparations are not so plentiful as we and you wish they were; but even a small supply goes a long way. Prices 4d. to 1/6.

Miss Patricia Roc, the famous young British Film Star.

Stay Pretty

△ In 1941, although beauty preparations were in short supply, advertisements such as this encouraged women to be feminine, beautiful and ready for anything. The message was: 'Don't neglect your looks!'
▷ Post-war advertisements became more risqué, as this one from 1947 shows.

es! It's Tattoo's secret...

is lip magic...this South Seas difference!

...no other lipstick is like it ... provocative ... ultra-
d ...glamour-laden. And ... lastingly, reassuringly,
nely unmoved by time, teacups, cocktails, kisses.
t's Tattoo's South Seas secret ... *stain* for lips instead
reasy coating! Never smearing ... no matter what!
Dawn-dewy ... dainty! You put it on ... let it set
wipe it off ... and only the lasting colour remains.

Daring shades ... enchanting as lagoon-side flowers
... NATURAL, TAHITI ROSE, TROPIC DAWN ... for the kiss
of the sun ... EXOTIC, HAWAIIAN, CORAL ... for romance that
steals in the dusk ... PAGAN RED, BLACK MAGIC, ORCHID.
Soul-stirring shades that thrill men's hearts ... now
doubly, trebly alluring with the *new* Tattoo Nailcote ... a
heavenly harmony of lips, nails, dress, mood, moment.

DRY SWIMMING

2 Do the Breast Stroke Dry Swim to build up the upper part of the chest. Stand with head erect, eyes looking straight ahead, arms raised as shown. Now swing arms slowly back on a line with shoulders. Finish by bending elbows and bringing hands back to position in front of chest, ready to move forward again.

5 The Side Stroke is fine for slimming heavy legs. Stretch right arm straight, sliding left arm up in front of chest until it reaches your face, then sweeping it down to hip. Right arm goes forward as left arm goes back to hip. Legs are opened and closed like scissors—under leg is bent back at knee, while upper leg goes forward with knee unbent. Reverse the motions on left side.

1 More oxygen in the lungs means greater vitality and joy of living. Fill the basin with water. Place a mirror at the bottom. Turn head to side as shown. Open mouth wide and take in a big gulp of air. Then turn face into the water, keeping eyes open, and breathe slowly out through the nose. Your eyes being open, you can of course see the air bubbles forming in the water.

22

The Body Beautiful

Hang your clothes on the back of a chair—and don't go

near the water, says a famous American

swimming authority, VICTOR LAWSON

YOU don't need to give up slimming even if you can't get near the sea-shore this year. Try Dry Swimming—the simple way to keep fit throughout the year.

Dry Swimming, this smart, modern method of streamlining the figure and building muscles, is sponsored by many doctors as a means of benefiting patients who are over-weight from inactivity, and of stimulating and re-developing tired muscles.

3 This is how you may practise the Breast Stroke Dry Swim with arms and legs together. Try this while lying across a bench. Bend legs back, keeping heels together. Then throw legs out—right leg to right side and left leg to left side—finishing with legs straight together.

4 Now try Dry Swimming the Crawl. Begin by walking briskly around the room, arms swinging vigorously. You are almost doing the Crawl. Now lie over on your bench. Move arms, alternately, forward and back to hip, and sway legs up and down, alternately, from the hips. Keep feet slightly pigeon-toed: this strengthens arches and ankles.

6 The English Relaxation position has been filmed under Mr. Lawson's direction for the Government, to demonstrate to war-workers this essential aid to health. Lie still in this position when you feel tired. In a few moments your tired muscles will relax, and you will feel refreshed.

7 Mr. Lawson's method of Dry Swimming the American Back Crawl was adopted by a Fifth Avenue beauty salon as a means of developing that good posture so sought after as an essential to beauty, poise and confidence.

Vary your strokes from day to day. Allow five minutes for each stroke.

23

△ Spreading figures were brought about by sedentary occupations and a stodgy diet, but with transport and travel curtailed, keeping fit was sometimes a problem. This article from 1944 provided one solution.

THE WAR –
Women's Role

The war years had a great impact on how the women left at home saw themselves. Pressed into service in the Land Army, as defence and factory workers, nurses and drivers, they became increasingly aware of their changing role in society. However, despite women's awareness of how capable and independent they could be, the man, whether at home or on leave from the war, still acted as head of the family. This opened the debate on the balance of power between the sexes – a debate that endures to this day.

The presence in the British Isles, from 1942, of the GIs led to many British women marrying American servicemen and *Good Housekeeping* was on hand to offer helpful advice to war brides. For others, social clubs, the cinema and dances were regular nights out, with Good Housekeeping advising on 'how to get on with Americans'. Other articles dealt with how to cope when loved ones returned, or, sadly, did not – the fear of many women left to wait.

SHE sets out shopping, past the ruined houses of her neighbours. She counts herself lucky. Her home suffered only minor damage from that same flying bomb—dark patched windows, doors that won't shut and ceilings that still fall every time a lorry passes the house. At any rate she has most of her roof. Thousands of London women have no roof at all. If your home is still intact, please show your gratitude in every way you can: by keeping your doors open a little longer to the homeless, by refraining from selfish shopping, and above all by trying sincerely to understand.

NAGGING away in the heart of thousands of women are two questions : " Will they come back ? " and " When they come home again, will they be changed ? "

Whether their loved ones are in the Services, evacuated, directed to war jobs or prisoners of war, there is a constant dread of change. To us women it is always unwelcome, since for us it so often means loss—of youth, of looks, of love. We must realise, however, that this question can have only one answer—a ringing, emphatic " Yes." All those who have been away from home will have changed, and changed radically. But this change can be the harbinger of a greatly enriched relationship, if we are prepared for it.

Repatriated prisoners of war and civilian internees have already shown some of the problems that can arise, and when demobilisation and the reorientation of industry really start, we shall meet many more. However, a difficulty understood is a difficulty half-conquered, and things will be much easier if we women who have remained at home try to realise what has happened to the character of those who have been away for years, with only a few brief, unreal leaves or holidays.

The fighting man will present the worst problem. There is no getting away from the fact that we who have stayed at home, no matter how much we have endured through privation and bombing, have not changed as much as he. Once a man joins up, he is at once deliberately isolated from civilian life, and locked up in the entirely different existence of the national fighting machine.

At one go he gives up his personality, his free will, his privacy, his personal belongings, his varied activities, his responsibilities as family man and citizen. He becomes a cog in the machine, taking orders without blinking, and obeying them instantly, eating, sleeping, and bathing in public, owning practically nothing except Service issue, following a whittled-down routine of " shooting and saluting " ; a mechanised man, trained to do one thing only— kill the enemy.

The thing which finally cuts the fighting man off from civilian life is the comradeship of a unique and wholly satisfying kind which his new world offers during every hour of the day.

When They Come Back

By Louise Morgan

" THE first morning he got here the Hunt turned up, and he was too upset to contain himself. That there were people at home who were content to spend money and time keeping horses and hounds, and using petrol in some cases, in the world of to-day, was beyond his comprehension. The thought of a fox being hunted was unbearable to him. He said ' It's like a prisoner of war facing a firing squad.' "

That was a repatriated prisoner, whose words typify to some extent the changed outlook of all those returning to ordinary civilian life. What can we do to make things easier for them ?

All the usual barriers—class, occupation, wealth, dress, religion, geographical origin—are down. Everything is shared on equal terms, men invent their own private language and their own secret mythology, as in the R.A.F.'s gremlins. The feeling of " belonging," of solidarity, gets in their blood, fires their imaginations.

Then, when they reach the front line, their sense of comradeship produces some of the finest flowers in the garden of humanity. Men give up their lives for each other. They experience over and over again the ecstasy of surviving mortal danger together. They sacrifice their comfort for a wounded comrade with all the tenderness of a mother for her child.

From these heights a man learns to scorn the petty competitions and jealousies of civilian life. His capacity for unselfish love and self-sacrifice is developed to a degree impossible in ordinary circumstances. This is what no woman must ever forget, for it marks the chief difference between her and the man who has come back to her from the front.

The shock will thus be great when he runs up against the cut-throat principle of civilian life—" each man for himself."

He will feel hurt, angry, profoundly homesick for what he has lost, and he will be in for a cynical period which may make him difficult to get along with and very unhappy in himself, if his family does not realise what he is experiencing, and give him constructive help. We can do this only by the warmest and most demonstrative possible response to his homecoming. I think your best guide might be to regard your husband or son as a boy home from school : for a while, you spoil him a bit, and it's good for him.

Then, when you have lapped him round with the comfort of your love and understanding, drawn out his whole story—if he wishes to tell it—and proved to him that he still " fits " into family life, you can safely begin to assert yourself a bit, to allow him to see that you, too, have been through it in your own way, but that you have developed, and are ready to build a new life with him.

Think of the task as an emergency engineering job. The black, swift river of wartime absence flows between you, and only you can bridge it. So you start your tough

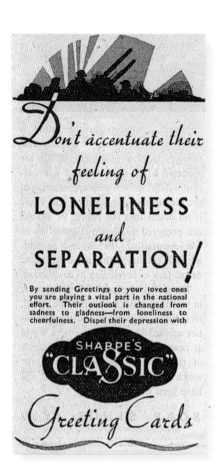
The Men in their Lives

◁ This 1945 article addresses the fears
of many women anticipating the return
from war of a loved one.

△ The advertisement above from 1941
encourages the sending of a greetings
card to sustain the spirits of servicemen
and POWs.

▷ A frank letter from a soldier to a
female 'camp follower' was reproduced
in the magazine in 1943.

Modern Vivandière

**An open letter from a soldier to a young woman—but we think
that the older women amongst us should read and ponder it, too**

● *This article is frank and it deals with a state of affairs that
is by no means pretty. Unfortunately, it's not rare. All of us
who are not afraid to face facts know that many girls in their
'teens, and nicely brought up girls, too, are infected with the
pitiful madness the writer describes.*

*What's to be done? It's natural that girls should want the
company of the opposite sex, but that mustn't mean lurking
at street corners and hanging round camps. Talk it over with
friends, and see what can be done in the way of group
hospitality for these young people. All that is wanted is a
lead; will you supply it?*

DEAR 1943 VIVANDIÈRE,
Quite probably you won't be surprised to hear from
me because you and I ought to know one another well.
I'm one of the chaps you've seen, for months past now,
coming out of the camp for an evening at the pictures, a
one-and-sixpenny hop or a couple of pints in the local.
You know me, don't you? I don't see how you could fail
to: you spend more time on sentry duty at the Gate than
anyone in barracks, and that's saying something. I ought
to know you, because, although I'm a pretty young soldier,
I've been acquainted with your sort, and worse, since I
clapped eyes on my first camp-follower at World's End
Camp, in Ballykinlar, in 1930. When you've read this letter
(which may look like so much harsh and uncalled-for
criticism) perhaps you'll see that I'm not just talking out
of turn, and that maybe I, and the fellows I'm spokesman
for, have got some sort of a reason for writing to you.
Well, I'm not a writing chap, but what I'm going to put
down comes to you straight up. It's one hundred per cent.,
so here goes:

I've addressed you as " 1943 Vivandière." Now I feel
that perhaps I couldn't do better than kick-off properly by
explaining what I mean under that term. Did you ever
hear about the vivandières of olden days, the women who
were camp-followers in the real sense of the word? They
travelled with an army, lived

The 'Little Woman'

△ ▷ Despite their changing roles
in society during the war, women
were still portrayed as deferring to
the man of the house, as the
advertisements above from 1947
show. The 1945 *Good Housekeeping*
cover is a particularly apt example.

APRIL 1945

GOOD HOUSEKEEPING

ONE SHILLING & SIXPENCE

Pearl Buck : C. Henry Warren : James Thurber

Louise Morgan on ADOPTION

"Catering for Two," by The Institute

Men CAN Cook

—an Airman says so

EVEN before the fly-bomb menace was reduced, many women came back from the evacuation areas because they were worried about how their husbands were managing without them. They imagined unsatisfactory, scratch meals; men waiting for their wives and a really good dinner. They need not have worried. If their menfolk did have scratch meals, it was lack of facilities or supplies that were to blame—not inability to take care of themselves.

For men make good cooks, often better cooks than women. To some of those " evacuation-widowers," evacuation meant the first change in diet for many years, for the first way in which men differ from the average woman in the kitchen is that they are not afraid to experiment.

Of course, you can argue that a wife who experiments in the kitchen, and whose experiment fails to turn out, is not likely to get the sympathetic consideration due to a pioneer from her husband. Perhaps not, but whatever the reason, women do like to stick to the well-beaten tracks when planning meals. This is not quite so true of men, who, looking through a cookery book, will have a shot at anything for which they have the necessary ingredients, even if they've never heard of it before.

That's another point. Having found the recipe, they stick to it. They work with the book open beside them, following the instructions item by item. Women have a habit of glancing through a recipe, then trusting to an inborn knack and a good memory to guide them when the operation starts. Not only that, they like to think out " improvements " of their own. " I'm sure that's not right," she says, backing her own experience against that of the author— and the result isn't quite what the author promised.

Men have been taught to do their jobs in the outside world systematically; it is a rule, for example, that a carpenter or radio-engineer goes out on a job with a complete tool kit. How many times have you seen a woman break off at a critical moment in her cooking to find a spoon or a bowl which a man, in nine cases out of ten, would have placed in readiness before he began ? And just as workmen take a pride in their tools, having them always in the pink of condition, they do wash up after them, so that at the end of one operation, everything is ready for the next.

What it all boils down to is that, generally speaking, men have been given a more scientific training than women. They have been compelled to take every (Continued on page 49)

The Age-old Debate

◁ The men have their say in this article from January 1945.
▷ As the men came back from the war trained in cooking, cleaning, washing and ironing, women were urged to let them share the household duties – an article from 1947.

should men do HOUSEWORK?

Do things go to pot when you're away or have to take to your bed?

If you split the burden of household chores now, your husband will know how to keep body, soul and shirts together in an emergency

A STORY is current that a certain British sergeant, returning from the wars, found his wife in the act of cleaning the windows.

"That's not the way to do it," he exclaimed in horror, taking the chamois-cloth out of her hand. "You use too much water!"

And forthwith he began to polish the window to high and beautiful transparency.

The poor wife fainted from shock! Resuscitated at length, she explained that never previously had she known her husband do a stroke of housework. Before the war he had, in fact, been so lazy that he had wanted her to blacken all the windows.

Possibly this story contains an element of exaggeration, but it does emphasise the fact that thousands of ex-Service men have returned home with unprecedented experience of the traditional feminine duties of washing, ironing, cleaning and cooking—qualified, as never before, to be true partners in the task of making a home. But are they gladly taking upon their newly trained shoulders an equitable share of housework? And if not, why not?

The fault, one man declares, lies with the women. "They always adopt the wrong tactics!"

If you want him to be a real 'partner in home-making' he advises:

1. Look for the job he can do better than you can. Frankly admit his greater success and don't be ashamed to learn from him.

2. Don't stand over him, always giving directions.

3. Don't ridicule and remember his mistakes.

4. If his sense of 'fairness' makes him share household tasks, go out of your way to help him with matters in which he is interested.

The Navy says 'YES!'

If you think the tale that men can do housework happily is too good to be true, read the post-war experiences of this mother of two sailors

ONCE upon a time I was proud mother of two small boys. But *what* boys! Untidy, dirty, always coming in from garden or fields and flinging down muddy shoes and torn coats anywhere and anyhow. My round of mending, washing and cleaning was unending.

Then came the war, and my two sons entered the Navy—the Service of all Services for teaching the things I had been unable to teach them, little ways that will make them welcome guests in any home without domestic staff.

Now mornings start well. The sons get up at first call or, better still, wake themselves and even get breakfast for me.

They make their beds, leave their rooms tidy, clothes in little piles (the Navy seems to love things in little rolled-up piles) and shoes left side by side like loving couples.

Washing-up is done in record time—knives, forks and spoons lined up in tidy rows and the wearisome task enlivened by good rollicking songs in which we all join.

They insist on washing their own clothes, or perhaps I should say doing their 'dhobi.' Ironing at any rate, I thought, (Continued on page 40)

Clubs—for grannies and 'teen-agers, for housewives and working girls—they're springing up all over the place. Our reporter believes these leisure-time clubs have come not only to stay, but to transform our social life

Members' Committee of a War Workers' Club

At all War Workers'

The canteen lounge of a Wolverhampton Club

Table tennis is popular at most types of clubs

A 2d. manicure is a feature of the Erdington Club

A Nee

NOTHING is mo symbolic of the kin of new world we a entering than the club which are springing u in thousands all over th country. Clubs, that i in the purely soci sense—not for " benefit," sport, politics or any othe specialised advantage, but simply for the purpose mixing with one's kind.

The club in this sense was not so long ago exclusiv to one sex in the wealthy and aristocratic " Clubland of the West End. Then the daring women pionee of the Emancipated Age started clubs of their own the fringes of Clubland—the Ladies' Carlton, Forun University Women's and so on.

But it is only recently, and especially since w

A Good Night Out

...ring is the favourite amusement

Every War Workers' Club has books and papers

Sunday tea is a "family" affair for the members

...ulfilled

By
Louise Morgan

started, that the club with no hint of uplift, patronage or charity, where one can meet friends, take meals, rest, amuse oneself and, in certain cases, have temporary residence, has extended to the whole community and every age, from children of seven to nonagenarians.

What is the cause of this extraordinary development? Fundamentally, it has sprung from the fact, established by the research of doctors, sociologists and biologists during the past twenty years, that no human being can be happy and healthy, or function as a citizen should, unless he has friendly contacts with his fellows. And the logical vehicle of such contacts is the social club.

Among the newest types of clubs are those for Old People. There were a few experimental ones before the war, notably the " Sons of Rest " in Birmingham, but since 1942 they have appeared in Sutton, Streatham, Teddington, Deptford, Lambeth and many other places. I visited one the other day which was started two years ago by the Social Service Department of St. Thomas's Hospital for its out-patients. It is known as the St. Thomas's Senior Club, and the house in Royal Street where it meets, across from the hospital, needs no number, for it is the only one left standing in the badly blitzed road.

Incredibly, these people who eke out a living on an average of about 19s. a week have already sent well over £100 to Russia, China and other needy places, by the sale of knitted garments, dishcloths, mops, aprons, lavender bags and toys, which they made from material costing a few pounds.

They were isolated and friendless, and some had been afraid they would lose the power of speech in

43

△ With the uncertainty over survival during the war years, class barriers were broken and clubs of all sorts sprang up, providing opportunities to socialize and, for a while, forget the worries of the conflict.

109

YOU have undertaken to become an American—just as millions of other people have done before you. Getting to know your adopted country will be an exciting adventure; the future is before you.

You have no doubt heard a good deal from your husband about the part of the United States where you will probably live, but you may still be wondering how you will get acquainted with people, what they will be like, and how you will manage your new home. This short guide cannot answer all your questions, but it may help you in making plans and in adjusting yourself to American ways of living.

Shyness: British and American

One thing you will notice when you meet people in America is that most of them will start a conversation without much hesitation. But when you think it over, you may feel that they have not really said much to let you into their lives. And perhaps you felt too shy to say much in return. Actually, most Americans are shy below the surface; they talk to cover it up and to make you feel their friendly intentions while they gradually get to know you. They won't be surprised if you are quiet. Smile, use your British habit of

Digest of a booklet prepared

Servicemen by Good

in conjunction with the Office of

slang—no one expects a newcomer to get them. Just laugh and admit you don't.

A great deal of American written humour is like your own, but there are some kinds of spoken humour that you must learn to take calmly. Exaggeration, of course, you know about, and learning the American language includes recognising what is true and what is too absurd to believe. Kidding is perhaps harder to get used to, but you have to learn. It may consist of mimicking to see if you "can take it."

The American Language

The first lesson in "American" concerns the names of things. You will learn these quickly, as the Americans had to do in Britain. Some words you will already have learned from your husband,

thanking people for everything, ask questions, and you will make people feel that you want to be friendly, too. In America it is good manners to praise anything you like, whether it is the food, the furniture or the view from the window. Dress your smartest for first interviews, and remember that, except in the smallest villages, lipstick is expected.

Listen, look around you, and take your time. Arm yourself with a few items of "small talk"—any odd fact about your voyage, what you have seen, where you have been, to cover your thoughts while you look about. Ask questions about simple things, where to shop, what to buy, what to do for entertainment. Everyone likes to lend a hand to a stranger, and people who have done you a small favour, and have been thanked with a smile, will like you from then on.

American Humour

Don't mind if at first you feel left out of some of the jokes that go by you in conversation. For one thing, most jokes in any country depend on some local topic or some peculiar twist of

and the rest you will soon acquire. Use the American names, so as not to be misunderstood. You need not use American slang words that are offensive in English, but if they are harmless in America, don't be bothered by them. Change your pronunciation if it causes misunderstanding—otherwise don't.

Manners

American manners, as you know, are different in various ways, some of which you may not like. The Americans do not say "thank you" in as many situations as the British, and they often ask a question without begging pardon. In American the word "sorry" is not as polite as "excuse me" or "I beg your pardon." A good rule is to watch how people talk to one another in your part of the country, and not to be surprised or offended if they do the same to you.

Reading Can Help

The other part of the American language that you need to learn is made up of facts about your part

6

War Brides

for British brides of American

Housekeeping Magazine,

War Information of the U.S.A.

of the country and the life of the people around you. When you know something of the history of your locality, where the people came from, and what they are interested in, you will begin to know what they are talking about and why they say such curious things.

The best way to start is by reading, because in reading you can learn without being embarrassed by not knowing what to ask. Take a local newspaper and read the local news until names and local events make sense in your mind. Go to the Public Library and talk with the librarian, if it is a small library, or the readers' adviser if it is a big one. The best and most painless way to learn about your new home from books is to read novels about your state and region, and then about America. At the library look over the women's household magazines. Subscribe to one

City Life

In a big city you can be as lonely as in any strange city in Britain, and if you live in a flat you won't have any neighbours.

But don't just sit down and die of home-sickness. There are ways of making friends even in New York or Chicago, but you have to be enterprising and self-reliant.

Wherever you find yourself, there are organisations that have open doors and expect strangers to come in on their own feet. The churches are still the principal ones. Then if you have belonged to the Red Cross or the Y.W.C.A. in Britain, you will find its opposite number in America. The church or the library can tell you about welfare societies, young people's societies and other groups or clubs catering for hobbies, according to your tastes. These clubs and societies want enthusiastic members who will join and do some of the work. You may as well find some congenial organisation and work with it, for this is one of the best ways to make real friends.

When you do get acquainted with people in a big city, entertaining will be somewhat different from what it is in a small town. People seldom "drop in," but couples often meet friends by arrangement for a dinner out, with a movie or

of them to help you on styles and ways of doing things about the house.

Making Friends—in a Small Town

You may find yourself settled far from your husband's family and surrounded entirely by strangers. In a small town the neighbours will call on you and try to be friendly. Neighbourliness is highly valued in America. They will chat with you when you are hanging out the laundry or digging in your garden—which probably will have no hedges around it.

If your neighbours call on you, be sure to return the call in a few days. Then you can invite them over for an evening. Home entertainment is simple in America: people sit on the porch in summer or in the living-room in winter, six or eight together, talking or playing cards. Light refreshments are served about ten o'clock—coffee and cake or iced ginger-ale and sandwiches, perhaps some candy or olives for decoration. Since refreshments are so simple, people often "drop in" without formality. For dinner, of course, invitations are necessary.

Illustrated by Tage Werner

theatre or dance afterwards. Cocktail parties before dinner are more frequent. Sunday trips to the country or the beach are a good excuse for inviting new friends to go along.

Sports are especially good links with other people. Incidentally, when you see American sports or take part in them, don't expect them to go by British rules. Sportsmanship is not a matter of what the rules are, but consists in playing by the rules and taking defeat gamely. One unwritten rule is that spectators may properly go quite wild and use violent language. Don't be shocked, it is all in fun! Americans, like the British, admire skill and pluck, and they particularly delight in anyone who can "take it" without showing any sign of distress.

Settling Down

Most Americans want more than anything else to settle down and have a home with children in it. But you will have to get used to what they mean by "settling down." It does not mean finding a secure job and a house and stopping there for ever. It (Continued on page 62)

7

△ In 1945 *Good Housekeeping* and the US Office of War Information compiled a booklet designed to help the thousands of British women who were marrying American servicemen.

HAVE you ever realised how much your mental outlook is reflected in your figure, and how much your figure depends for gracefulness on the way you think?

For instance, when you feel tired or depressed your figure shows it with a slumped waistline, a droopy hang of the head. But when you feel on top of the world, up goes your head, back go your shoulders and the muscles all over your body are under better control.

Undoubtedly, if we could always feel that all was right with the world, there would be few figure faults to bother us. But that is not so easy, especially in these days of strain and anxiety. As a consequence, many of us are developing bad posture habits which are doing unattractive things to our figures.

The only girls and women who seem to be escaping them are those in the Services. They are lucky in having regular physical training, but the main and lasting benefits come from wearing a uniform. There's something about a uniform which makes you figure-conscious. The sparse cut simply reminds you to hold yourself upright and swing from the hips when you walk, instinct tells you that to slouch or slump ruins the effect. It would be a fine thing for our silhouettes, if we all put ourselves mentally into uniform and carried ourselves accordingly.

What happens to a figure when it is habitually carried as if it were in uniform? What benefits does it receive?

First of all, an upright carriage pulls all the muscles upwards from the waist. This means diaphragms stop that loose, careless bulging; busts do not get such a chance to droop. Instead, the main muscles which control their firmness, called the pectoral muscles, which lie just below the shoulders, are pulled into line and do their proper job of supporting. Your neckline also improves, because your head goes into proper alignment. There's no chance of its hanging forward so that your chin pokes out.

The rest of the figure receives just as many benefits. The stomach muscles are lifted, instead of being allowed to stand at the easy all day long, and consequently lose their strength. The lower part of the back stays tucked in and, as you walk, your legs move rhythmically from the thighs and you

SUSAN DRAKE tells you how to smarten up your appearance without diet, exercises, extra make-up or even new clothes!

no longer jerk them forward fro the knees in ugly, ageing litt steps. The whole balance of t figure is correct, so that the wo of your muscles is evenly di tributed.

Just test this out for yourself shoes with reasonable heels, without shoes. Stand straight, n rigidly, but simply comfortabl with your arms at yo side. Now imagi you are in uniform You want the skirt set well, the tunic fit smoothly across t shoulders. You don want any line to sti out at the back. pull yourself upwar from the waist. If y think, "Oh dear, th is going to be strain!" it is hig time you resolute made such a posture habit, because yo figure, whatever yo age may be, is losi its pliability, natural gift for contro

Hold the position for a minute, the relax if you must, but take it again. This is a very simple exe cise, but it is a basic one for acquiri figure control on which gracefulne and a youthful line depend. Then ju walk. Notice how your legs move a long, fluid line.

If you would only cultivate th muscle control until it is second natu you would soon see an immense in provement in your figure, and y would feel better as well. So ma digestive disorders come from faul posture. This is because the orga are cramped and cannot do their wo properly.

Keep a watch on yourself when y sit. There's a way of sitting whi instantly wins admiration, and the is another way which makes an o server think, "Oh, how clumsy a untidy!" It's the first way th keeps your figure youthful. Nobod except perhaps a very old or infir person, should have to scramble o of a chair or let herself flop unconto lably into one. Sitting, like walkin should be fluid, easy and economic in action.

How do you sit? Your back shou be against (Continued on page 7

Put Your

FIGURE *into* UNIFORM

A DAY IN THE LIFE OF MRS FECKLESS

10.00 a.m. Clears out larder and discovers that the stale bread that was to be made into rusks has gone mouldy and has to be thrown away. Decides that the bone from the joint had better be burnt, in case it should "go off," too. "Anyway, it's so small I can't see what good it could be!"

10.20 a.m. Rings up sister-in-law in Devon and arranges to go there for a week-end while the weather is still nice.

10.45 a.m. Peels vegetables for lunch and wraps peelings in newspaper before putting them out for pig-food collector.

12.10 p.m. Looks over fence at neighbour, who is busy in vegetable plot, and remarks, "I'm afraid I'm not very patriotic—I prefer flowers to vegetables."

12.30 p.m. Opens can of meat for lunch and, without bothering to remove the paper wrapper from the can, throws it in the dustbin with the ashes from the kitchen boiler, the tea leaves, etc.

1.45 p.m. Finds that a rubber has come off the heel of her shoe, so adds this to the collection in the dustbin, saying, "Oh, they can sort it out, and anyway, if you do separate the stuff, the men only mix it up again."

2.30 p.m. Goes up to town and buys a stock of stationery and three linen table-cloths, although she still has several left, because they won't be available much longer. Finds she has forgotten her shopping basket, so gets shop to enter the goods and deliver them. Buys "such a lovely handbag, though it *was* rather expensive!"

5.00 p.m. Goes home, rather annoyed to find the train full up with office workers, etc., and no seat available for herself.

5.45 p.m. Reaches home, and finds that she has missed (a) the neighbour who calls weekly with National Savings stamps; and (b) the Boy Scouts to whom she had promised her waste paper.

6.30 p.m. Transfers articles from her old handbag to the new one, to use it for bridge party to-morrow, and burns all the odd bits of paper and letters, etc., that she no longer wants.

Mrs. FECKLESS

has committed a

number of "crimes" against

the national weal.

Tell us what they are, and

what she should have

done instead to have spent a

patriotic day.

Five prizes of 10/- worth

of National Savings Stamps for

the five best answers.

Closing date July 17th.

Send to the

Competition Editor,

Good Housekeeping,

28/30 Grosvenor Gardens,

London, S.W.1

◁ By June 1941 over 100,000 women were in the services and by the end of that year full conscription of women was introduced. This article from 1942 extols the benefits to posture that wearing a uniform can give.

△ This 1942 quiz reminds readers of their patriotic duties.

Do the Right Thing

Bouquet for the Forces

Paper for these weapons was presented to the Forces—via the local Salvage Collectors—by Mrs. Smith, of Britishtown. What have you given this week? Remember—

YOUR WASTE PAPER IS A MUNITION OF WAR

N.B.—Mrs. Smith gave sufficient paper for: Cups and tubes for the charges in the bomb and the mine; Rings, wads, washers, and cups for two shells; Cartridge wads for aero-cannon shells and small-arm cartridges, also paper for one box for ·303 cartridges—in other words, an old A.B.C., the week's newspapers, and the unwanted books and magazines from the sitting-room

The
WAR EFFORT

The overwhelming theme of the war effort was save, salvage and sacrifice – paper and cardboard in any form was collected for recycling into items such as rifle cartridges, log books and maps; meat, but not fish, bones were used for making explosives, and rubber, tins, string and rags were just some of the other items collected. Paper rationing meant that *Good Housekeeping*, along with other publications, had to reduce their size, but they published throughout the war, providing help and support, as well as entertainment in the form of fiction and light-hearted articles.

The conservation of national energy resources was paramount and, with many miners in the services, coal was in short supply. Among the economy measures called for was to sieve the cinders and bank the fire with items such as potato peelings, ashes, or cans filled with tea leaves. When petrol was banned for personal use in 1943 the nation took to public transport, cycling or walking.

"RAT! TAT! TAT!"

Ratta! Tat! Tat! "Registered letter. Sign here, please! Hope your Ma's better. 'Flu can be dangerous at her age . . ." Yes, a postman yesterday . . . but today, knocking at the Hun's door — with steel bullets. Rat! tat! tat! Knocking 'em out of their positions with deadly machine gun fire. Helping to give the knock-out to Nazism. We salute him! We Salute the Soldier! And by saving more . . . very much more . . . we can show our heartfelt gratitude for all that he is doing.

SALUTE THE SOLDIER

Issued by the National Savings Committee

"PASS DOWN THE BUS, PLEASE!"

A voice rasps out . . . "Action Stations! Number one, GO!" Charlie's number two. He leans across to his pal. "A threepenny to Bethnal Green! Pass down the bus, please!" His pal grins. Charlie was a conductor. Now it's Charlie's turn. "Number two, GO!" Charlie's off. Salute his daring! Salute the Soldier. Salute with more savings! We can all do this. We *must* do it. Let us cut our spending and increase our lending — and so help in a practical way to Salute the Soldier!

SALUTE THE SOLDIER

Issued by the National Savings Committee.

△ The National Savings Campaign had begun in 1939, but in 1944 a new drive was launched by the National Savings Committee with 'Salute the Soldier', to encourage people to continue to save as much money as they could to 'help the boys out there'.

"REPAIR SQUAD, PLEASE!"

Yesterday . . . in the garage . . . repairing cars . . . "a little trouble with the plugs, sir ? Soon get that fixed !" Today a soldier—Right in the thick of it . . . shells bursting . . . snipers taking a crack at him. But he does it ! And repairs another tank — ready for action ! Salute his toughness — his endurance !

Salute the Soldier — with more savings ! Let us all vow today to mobilize our money — by cutting spending and increasing lending. Let us lend to our country — and so lend practical help to "the boys out there !"

SALUTE THE SOLDIER

Issued by the National Savings Committee

> "We shall not flag or fail, we shall go on to the end. We shall fight on the seas and oceans, we shall fight with growing confidence and growing strength in the air. We shall defend our Island, whatever the cost may be ; we shall fight on the beaches, we shall fight on the landing grounds, we shall fight in the fields and in the streets, we shall fight in the hills. We shall never surrender."
>
> RT. HON. WINSTON CHURCHILL, M.P.

Builders of Democracy

How can we praise Churchill — adequately? For he is the centre of our hopes, the symbol of our determination, the spearhead of our ever-growing power. When the smoke of battle has cleared away we shall see even more clearly how much the whole world owes to him. *His example has inspired free men to stand fast for their freedom against Nazidom.* What greater praise could there be?

Issued by the manufacturers of

J. B. LEWIS AND SONS LIMITED NOTTINGHAM ESTABLISHED 1815

MERIDIAN
DOUBLE LOCK

SUPPLIERS TO THE WHOLESALE TRADE

△ Winston Churchill symbolized the British spirit.

Saluting the Soldier

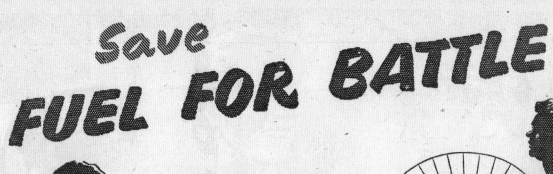

Save FUEL FOR BATTLE

says
FUEL WATCHER

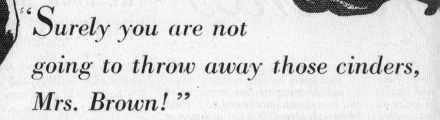

"Surely you are not going to throw away those cinders, Mrs. Brown!"

"Oh no — I have always found them better than c
for lighting the fire."

"It isn't only that — it's also a question of saving burna.
fuel. Do you know that if cinders were properly used in every househo
the home coal consumption of the country would be *750,000 tons less ea
year?"

"Good gracious! I had no idea that it was so important. Now I really
glad that I have always saved cinders."

*REMEMBER that 750,000 tons of coal are used in producing the steel
making 10 battleships.

ISSUED BY THE MINISTRY OF FUEL AND POW

FUEL COMMUNIQUE

ACTIVE SERVICE on 12,000,000 Fronts

Britain's 12,000,000 households are 12,000,000 battle fronts in this great drive to save fuel. Each one counts. Each one must do its part. An *active* part, for it isn't enough to stop wasting coal or gas or electricity or paraffin; there must be *economies* in the use of fuel in all its forms.

So much depends on Women

Housewives, you have done splendidly so far—you have put hearts into this great effort to help the war effort. Colder we makes the struggle harder for you now—*but keep it up*. Put you to work as well as your will-power and plan your own specia of saving.

YOU CAN DO IT—

Save a fire one or two nights a week by sharing with friends and neighbours.

Save coal or coke when using the oven or boiler by banking the fire up with slack. This prevents cold air entering.

Save on your gas fire by not turning it full on; or if you have an electric

heater which has two or r use only one.

Save in cooking by using gas ring instead of the larg

Save hot water by never than 5 inches in the ba doing the day's washi one time.

KEEP YOUR EYE ON YOUR FUEL

5 lbs. OF COAL SAVED IN ONE DAY BY 1,500,000 HOMES WILL PROVIDE ENOUGH FUEL TO BUILD A DESTROYER

NOTE: 5 lbs. of coal are used in 2 hours by a gas fire or electric oven.

Is YOUR home helping to build a destroyer?

Save FUEL for BATTLE

ISSUED BY THE MINISTRY OF FUEL AND POWER

H—6   48

◁ △ The Ministry of Fuel and Power issued regular Fuel Communiques during the war reminding people of their duty to save fuel in all its forms. These date from early 1944. Advice included the instruction to bathe in no more than five inches of water.

Cinders Save the Day

Paper for munitions of war, and for everyday use, can be made in two ways : from fresh raw material, largely wood pulp, or from second-hand re-pulped paper.

Wood pulp is a bulky cargo, and with ships a crying need for all kinds of war transport, urgent munitions, as well as such civilian essentials as cartons, tickets, stationery, newspapers, books, magazines, and so on, are overwhelmingly dependent on supplies of pulped paper.

W·H·SMITH & SON

Have you an empty box – or two ?

The first would be for the papers that your newsagent delivers— in those districts where messengers can still be obtained. If each customer, especially in the country and where houses are set well back from the road, would fix a newspaper box at his gate so that the delivery boy need not go right up to the front door, some rounds could be stretched a little and a few more people relieved of the trouble of fetching their own papers.

The second box we have in mind —or better still a depot—is for collecting and passing on papers and magazines when they are done with. Newsagents cannot very well undertake this work themselves, for obvious reasons, but none know better than they how many people are going without because of paper-rationing. Hospitals, and men and women in the Forces, would particularly appreciate a good neighbourly action such as this. Please share your newspapers and magazines before they are salvaged.

Share your papers and magazines before they are salvaged

Precious Paper

△ ▷ Once the war started, salvaging paper became a national pastime and salvage shops were opened across the country. Bought goods were no longer wrapped and books, bills, postcards and even bus tickets were assiduously collected for recycling.

EVERY WOMAN
A MUNITION WORKER

Paper is one of
the most urgently needed
war supplies:
have YOU
contributed
your
fair share?

[P.T.O

URN THE ... DOWN
AND THROW OUT YOUR SAL **V** AGE

Francina Sorabji

P. Cornell

HOUSEWIVES SAVE YOUR SALVAGE

SAL **V** AGE FOR VICTORY

Mary Greene

SALVAGE SPEEDS THE BOMBER

Ronald McRae

CHILDREN'S SALVAGE COMPETITION

THE entries in this contest were so good that we decided to increase the number of prizes in each class, as given in the lists on this page. We illustrate a few of those designs which end themselves best to reproduction.

THEY RISK THEIR LIVES FOR YOU BUT **YOU** TOO CAN HELP WIN THROUGH
SO RALLY BOYS AND GIRLS COLLECT WASTE PAPER ETC. IT IS VITALY NEEDED TO PRODUCE SHELL CONTAINERS, ETC

Alex Leit—

NEWS FROM THE SALVAGE FRONT

Paper: As you will have read in your daily papers, the supply of Waste Paper has fallen off sadly—people are throwing it away and even destroying it, instead of hoarding every single little scrap for salvage. How is *your* conscience on this point?

It isn't just a whim of the Government, you know, to cause you more trouble—it's an urgent necessity to salvage all the paper possible. If we fail to do it, we're breaking faith with our men and women in the Services. The country can't continue to equip them properly unless the supply of Waste Paper increases and maintains a high level. What about it? Are you going to go through the boxroom and your desk again, to turn out everything you can spare, and are you going to hang up a bag or box in which the family can place every scrap of unwanted paper as it comes to hand?

Contraries: This intriguing word means all the waste materials other than paper which still find their way into bundles of waste paper. You'd be surprised at the variety of contraries which turn up, and usually just where they can do most damage—in the valuable machinery of the mills where the waste paper is processed.

It probably wouldn't occur to you to put worn-out boots and shoes or dead animals or glass bottles into your waste paper, but some people have done so. Possibly, though, you have committed the commonest sin of all—allowed the metal top of a scouring powder container to go into your waste paper, along with the cardboard sides. Do remember to put the metal separate from the paper: both are valuable, but metal in the wrong place does more harm than good—it may put a machine out of work for days.

Bones: Far too many bones are still wasted, and we have to import what should come from our own households.

Of course, it's a little trouble to clean them, dry them off (in the oven after the gas has been turned out, or on top of the stove), and then put them in a metal container with a loosely fitting lid. But fighting is quite a lot of trouble, too, and winning this war is bound to mean a lot of trouble for all of us. Won't you accept this task cheerfully? You've done so well in many other ways—don't fall down on the job now.

P.S.—Fish bones are not wanted.

Books: A special effort is being made to obtain books for the Services to read; for restocking blitzed libraries; and for repulping for munitions.

Your own town or district will doubtless be having a drive sooner or later. Please support it as well as you can—you may be assured that any books you give will be examined by experts, so that they can be directed where they will do the country most good.

Salvage Stewards: Excellent results have been obtained, but more Stewards are needed.

If by any unlikely chance you are still looking for a piece of National Service to do at home, why not volunteer for this job? Get in touch with your Local Authority for details.

* Count your coupons—they have a long way to go!

◁ Children were also encouraged to do their bit for the country and *Good Housekeeping* ran this competition in March 1943.

△ The public seem to have been flagging in their salvaging efforts, as this bulletin later in 1943 reminds them.

Salvage – your Duty

Longer Life for your TOWELS

A GREAT DEAL of the cotton and linen that used to be made into towels is needed now for sterner tasks—needed badly. Here are some hints on how to get extra wear out of the towels you have, so that you may keep down your purchases of new towels.

ABOUT BATH TOWELS

Worn bath towels can be cut up and hemmed to make two or three small hand or face towels (badly worn bits will do for dusters, floor cloths, etc.). Beach robes, little used nowadays, will often make a good sized bath towel. When darning any towelling, use an oddment of wool, leaving the usual loops. When the towel is washed, the wool will thicken a trifle and be almost unnoticeable.

FACING UP TO IT

Face towels that get beyond patching can be quilted together—two thin ones, joined with diamond stitching, make a towel that will give you good wear, or a single towel doubled over and stitched makes a hand or kitchen towel.

KITCHEN TOWEL TACTICS

A badly worn roller towel will provide material for at least one glass cloth. Discarded pillow cases or the odd bits of old sheets make excellent tea towels. Old bags used for dog biscuits or preserving sugar also make tea towels when unpicked and hemmed. Wash all kitchen towels regularly so that they will not need hard rubbing and boiling, which wears them out. Sew loops on your towels to hang them up by—it helps them last longer. And towels can be used less if dishes are well rinsed and left to drain and dry themselves.

WHILE WE'RE IN THE KITCHEN—a word about saucepans and kettles, as new ones are in short supply. *Soak* pots clean instead of scraping or scouring them too vigorously. If a pan gets burnt, pour in a cupful of cold water and leave it to soak for 24 hours. Then clean in the ordinary way. If you have iron or tin utensils dry them very carefully to avoid rust. To keep a tin kettle rust free, always empty it after use and stand it upside down to drain.

JOIN A MAKE DO AND MEND CLASS

Sewing and household jobbery classes and mending parties are being formed all over the country. Already there are hundreds of them in full swing. Any Citizens' Advice Bureau will be glad to tell you where and when your nearest class or party meets, and how you can join or help to form one in your own district.

Mend & make do to save buying new

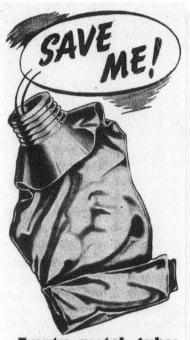

Empty metal tubes
needed *URGENTLY!*

HELP to relieve the drain on the Nation's reduced metal supplies. Hand all empty collapsible metal tubes to your retailer. Remember —tubes of all kinds are wanted at once. The metal is urgently needed and will be sold for the benefit of the Red Cross and St. John Fund.

GIVE YOUR EMPTY METAL TUBES AND HELP THE

RED CROSS & ST. JOHN

This space has been presented by Phillips' Dental Magnesia.

ISSUED BY THE DENTIFRICE
MANUFACTURERS OF GREAT BRITAIN

HE HATES TO SEE CLOTHES DOING EXTRA WAR SERVICE

This kind of war work drives the Squander Bug wild! Don't listen to him . . . keep right on with it. You'll be as proud as punch of your 'creations'—no cash or coupons required. Now you will be able to buy more Savings Certificates . . . no wonder the Squander Bug hates that sewing machine!

Savings Certificates costing 15/- are worth 20/6 in 10 years— increase free of income tax. They can be bought outright or by instalments with 6d., 2/6 or 5/- Savings Stamps through your Savings Group or Centre or at any Post Office or Trustee Savings Bank. Buy Now!

ISSUED BY THE NATIONAL SAVINGS COMMITTEE

◁ Recycling and making do and mending was the theme of many Board of Trade notices, such as this one from 1943.
△ Metal was urgently needed and even empty toothpaste tubes could be reused; however, the Squander Bug laughed at your efforts.

Recycle!

Donations Please

△ ▷ Organisations such as the Salvation Army and the Red Cross relied on donations from the public to help them help others during the war. With the Order of St John. the Red Cross sent out 20 million food parcels to the troops and prisoners of war. and aided the sick and wounded needing help as a result of enemy action.

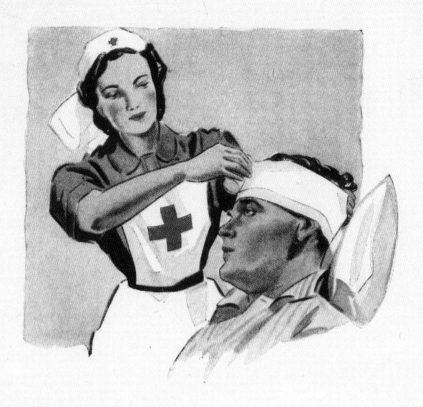

Somewhere, someone is depending *personally* on the help you give to the Red Cross. He may be a wounded soldier in a far-off land, or a prisoner of war waiting for a parcel, or an interned civilian needing aid. Wherever he is and whatever his plight you cannot let him down . . . . this should be the resolution for each and everyone of us—to give a little more to the Red Cross and to give it regularly.

This Appeal is made by **joyce** (CALIFORNIA) Ltd.